OSHO® TRANSFORMATION TAROT

St. Martin's Press
NEW YORK

OSHO TRANSFORMATION TAROT

For information, address:
St. Martin's Press
175 Fifth Avenue
New York, NY 10010

Cover art by Osho
Original illustrations by Pujan
Edited by Sarito
Commentaries by Osho
Design and typeset by Bullet Liongson

ISBN 0-312-24530-0

First Edition
10 9 8 7 6 5 4 3 2 1

Tremendous is the splendor of a person who has come to know everything that goes on within him, because by being aware, all that is false disappears and all that is real is nourished.

Except this, there is no radical transformation possible.

No religion can give it to you, no messiah can give it to you.

It is a gift that you have to give to yourself.—OSHO

The cards of the Osho Transformation Tarot are tools for self-discovery. Each card points the way to an opening for renewal and change that is available to each of us if we can only learn to become more aware of our own hidden potential. Each parable contains a priceless insight that provokes us to search for the truth within ourselves, and nourish it with the gift of our own awareness.

The source of these cards and their accompanying text lies in the eternal thread that unites all of the world's great wisdom traditions. Stories from the ecstatic path of the Sufis are matched by the earthy parables of Zen; the passion and love of Jesus is complemented by the purity and wisdom of the Buddha. And because the profound truths of these great traditions are contained in simple stories and parables, they go deep into our hearts. We can remember them easily and see them reflected in the events of our everyday lives. As we come to know and understand the characters in each story we can see their sorrows and their joys as mirrors of our own. Slowly, we begin to unravel all the inner "shoulds" and "shouldn'ts" that have governed us up to now. And once we have freed ourselves of this burden we discover the open inner space that is the soil where real transformation takes root and grows.

The Osho Transformation Tarot can be used in a number of ways. You can choose one card and read the accompanying story as a theme for contemplation during the day. Or, you can arrange several cards in any of the simple layouts suggested in this book, to gain insight into a particular life question that is facing you right now.

Change should come from the innermost core, it should not come from the periphery. And all turmoil is on the periphery; deep down there is no turmoil. You are just like the sea—go and watch the sea—all the turmoil, all the waves clashing, is just on the surface. But as you go deep, the deeper you go there is more and more calm. At the deepest part of the sea there is no turmoil, not a single wave.

First go deeper into your inner sea so you achieve a calm crystallization, so you achieve the point where no disturbance ever reaches. Stand there. From there every change comes, every transformation comes. Once you are there you have become a master of yourself.—OSHO

Using the Osho Transformation Tarot can be a form of meditation. Whether you are choosing cards for yourself or conducting a reading for another person, taking a little time for preparation beforehand is essential. Find a quiet space where you will not be disturbed. Allow yourself to settle into a relaxed and open attitude as you shuffle the cards, emptying the mind of all preconceived ideas you might have about the answer to your question or concern. Let go of any other preoccupations that might distract your attention from the reading. Once you feel settled and relaxed, then spread the deck face down in a fan and choose your card or cards.

As you look at the cards you have chosen, remember that the words are just indicators toward the larger message and insight contained in the corresponding story or parable. Even seemingly "negative" words point the way to a hidden potential for transformation and greater understanding. This will become clear as you read the stories illustrated by the cards.

Finally, remember Osho's message to remain playful and lighthearted about all aspects of your search, both inner and outer. He says, "Take life joyfully, take life easily, take life relaxedly, don't create unnecessary problems. Ninety-nine percent of your problems are created by you because you take life seriously. Seriousness is the root cause of problems. Be playful... be alive, be abundantly alive. Live each moment as if this is the last moment. Live it intensely; let your torch burn from both sides together. Even if it is only for one moment, that is enough. One moment of intense totality is enough to give you the taste of eternity."

Here are some simple spreads that can be used in your readings.

1. **Meditation for the Day**
   Choose just one card, without holding any particular question in your mind. Read the story and absorb it as deeply as you can, so you can keep it with you throughout the day. You might want to carry the card as a reminder. Take notice of events that happen during the day that might be related to the message or insight given by the card.

2. **Relating**

This spread can be used to gain insight into your relationship with another person, whether that person is a friend, lover or business associate.

1	2
3	4

After shuffling the cards and spreading them into a fan, choose a total of four cards.

1. The first card will represent you and what you bring to the relationship, or what lessons it has to teach you.
2. The second represents the other person and what he or she brings to the relationship.
3. The third card represents the dynamics of the relationship itself, the quality or flavor of the interaction between the two of you.
4. The fourth and final card represents the enlightened insight into the relationship, and contains the key to its highest potential.

3. **Inner and Outer—The Simple Cross**

Osho speaks about the cross as a symbol for the inner and outer dimensions of being—the horizontal line of time and events in the outside world, and the vertical line of growth from unconscious habits and assumptions to conscious awareness. This spread provides an "in-the-moment" reading of both these dimensions, and how they are influencing your life right now.

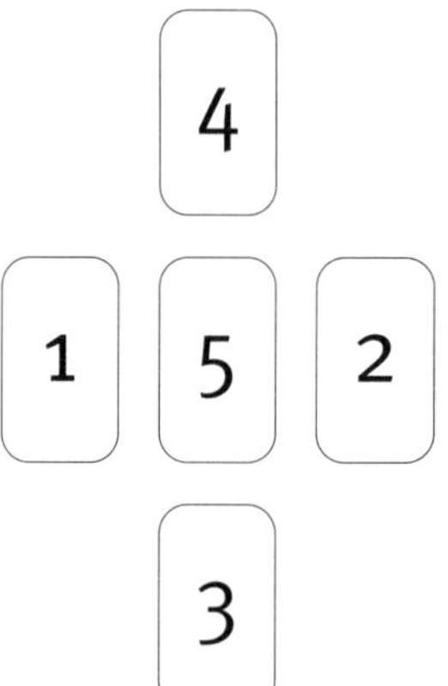

Choose five cards, as follows:

1. The first card is placed at the beginning of the horizontal line, and represents recent events and circumstances in your life. It may also represent outer influences affecting you or your question, that you might not be fully aware of.
2. The second card is placed at the end of the horizontal line and represents either the direction that outer events are taking, or external influences that you are aware of.
3. Card three is placed at the foot of the cross and represents inner influences or qualities that you might not be aware of—in other words, the seed of transformation that is now preparing to take root within you.
4. Card four is placed at the top, and signifies the direction of growth in your inner awareness, or new levels of understanding that are just now becoming available to you.
5. The last card is placed in the center, and represents the key to integrating the horizontal and vertical dimensions of your life. It can also symbolize the inner understanding that is most important for you to work on right now.

4. **Choiceless Awareness**

This spread is helpful in examining all the elements of a choice between two alternatives, and the hidden potential that lies within each. NOTE: The first card you choose should be left face down until all the other cards have been chosen and viewed.

1. Choose one card and place it face down on the left.
2. Choose three cards for "alternative A" and place them face up, as shown in the diagram.
3. Now choose three cards for "alternative B" and place them face up.

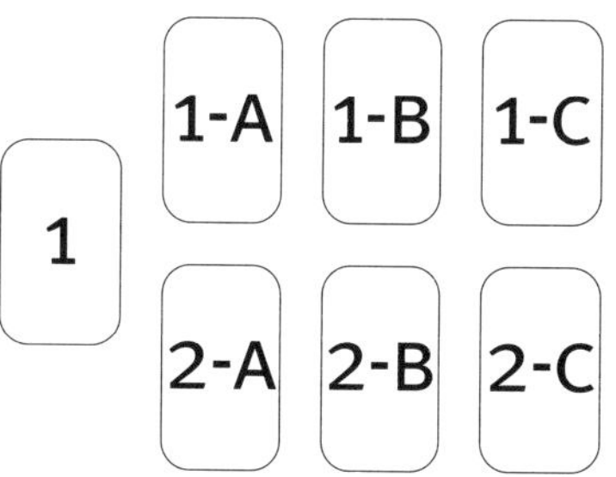

The first card in each line represents the challenges and opportunities available to the mind, should you make this choice. It answers the question, "What new intellectual understanding or intellectual creativity will become available to me should I make this choice?" The second represents the emotional influences arising out of each decision—what will happen in the world of feelings—and the third card of "manifestation" indicates what broader changes in your life or understanding are likely to result as a consequence of your choice in each case.

4. Once you have looked into the implications of the two alternatives, turn the first card over for an insight into what the "choiceless choice" might be.

No-Mind

The state of no-mind is the state of the divine. God is not a thought but the experience of thoughtlessness. It is not a content in the mind; it is the explosion when the mind is content-less. It is not an object that you can see; it is the very capacity to see. It is not the seen but the seer. It is not like the clouds that gather in the sky, but the sky when there are no clouds. It is that empty sky.

When the consciousness is not going out to any object, when there is nothing to see, nothing to think, just emptiness all around, then one falls upon oneself. There is nowhere to go—one relaxes into one's source, and that source is God.

No-Mind

The Ultimate and the Inexpressible

Your inner being is nothing but the inner sky. The sky is empty, but it is the empty sky that holds all, the whole existence, the sun, the moon, the stars, the earth, the planets. It is the empty sky that gives space to all that is. It is the empty sky that is the background of all that exists. Things come and go and the sky remains the same.

In exactly the same way, you have an inner sky; it is also empty. Clouds come and go, planets are born and disappear, stars arise and die, and the inner sky remains the same, untouched, untarnished, unscarred. We call that inner sky *sakshin*, the witness—and that is the whole goal of meditation.

Go in, enjoy the inner sky. Remember, whatsoever you can see, you are not it. You can see thoughts, then you are not thoughts; you can see your feelings, then you are not your feelings; you can see your dreams, desires, memories, imaginations, projections, then you are not them. Go on eliminating all that you can see. Then one day the tremendous moment arrives, the most significant moment of one's life, when there is nothing left to be rejected. All the seen has disappeared and only the seer is there. That seer is the empty sky.

To know it is to be fearless, and to know it is to be full of love. To know it is to be God, is to be immortal.

There is no way of contaminating the sky, of making impressions on it, marks on it. We can draw lines on water, but no sooner are the lines made than they disappear; yet if lines are made on stone they last for thousands of years. Lines just cannot be drawn in the sky, so there is no question of their disappearing. Please understand this difference. Lines cannot be drawn in the sky—I may move my finger across the sky, the finger passes but the line is not drawn and the question of the disappearance of the line simply does not arise.

The day a person goes beyond the mind, when the consciousness transcends the mind, he experiences that, like the sky, so far no marks or lines have ever been drawn on the soul. It is eternally pure, eternally enlightened, no pollution has ever happened to it.

Communion

Man is living as an island, and that's where all misery arises. Down the centuries man has been trying to live independently from existence—that is not possible in the very nature of things. Man can neither be independent nor dependent. Existence is a state of interdependence: everything depends on everything else. There is no hierarchy, nobody is lower and nobody is higher. Existence is a communion, an eternal love affair.

But the idea that man has to be higher, superior, special, creates trouble. Man has to be nothing—man has to dissolve into the totality of things. And when we drop all the barriers, communion happens and that communion is a benediction. To be one with the whole is all. That is the very core of religiousness.

Communion

Harmony Without and Within

Heraclitus says: It would not be better if things happened to men just as they wish. Unless you expect the unexpected you will never find the truth, for it is hard to discover and hard to attain. Nature loves to hide. The lord whose oracle is at Delphi neither speaks nor conceals—but gives signs.

Existence has no language... and if you depend on language there can be no communication with existence. Existence is a mystery, you cannot interpret it. If you interpret, you miss. Existence can be lived, but not thought about. It is more like poetry, less like philosophy. It is a sign, it is a door. It shows, but it says nothing. Through mind, there is no approach to existence. If you think about it, you can go on thinking and thinking, about and about, but you will never reach it—because it is precisely thinking that is the barrier. Thinking is a private world, it belongs to you—then you are enclosed, encapsulated, imprisoned within yourself. Nonthinking, you are no more; you are enclosed no more. You open, you become porous, existence flows into you and you flow into existence.

Learn to listen—listening means you are open, vulnerable, receptive, but you are not in any way thinking. Thinking is a positive action. Listening is passivity: you become like a valley and receive; you become like a womb and you receive. If you can listen, then nature speaks—but it is not a language. Nature doesn't use words. Then what does nature use? Says Heraclitus, it uses signs. A flower is there: what is the sign in it? It is not saying anything—but can you really say it is not saying anything? It is saying much, but it is not using any words—a wordless message.

To hear the wordless you will have to become wordless, because only the same can hear the same, only the same can relate to the same.

Sitting by a flower, don't be a person, be a flower. Sitting by the tree, don't be a person, be a tree. Taking a bath in a river, don't be a man, be a river. And then millions of signs are given to you. And it is not a communication—it is a communion. Then nature speaks, speaks in thousands of tongues, but not in language.

Enlightenment

Whatsoever you do, do it with deep alertness; then even small things become sacred. Then cooking or cleaning become sacred; they become worship. It is not a question of what you are doing, the question is how you are doing it. You can clean the floor like a robot, a mechanical thing; you have to clean it, so you clean it—then you miss something beautiful. Cleaning the floor could have been a great experience—you missed it; the floor is cleaned but something that could have happened within you has not happened. If you were aware, alert, not only the floor but you yourself would have felt a deep cleansing.

Clean the floor full of awareness, luminous with awareness. Work or sit or walk, but one thing has to be a continuous thread: make more and more moments of your life luminous with awareness. Let the candle of awareness burn in each moment, in each act. The cumulative effect is what enlightenment is. The cumulative effect, all the moments together, all small candles together, become a great source of light.

3

Enlightenment

Why the Buddha Waits at the Gates of Paradise

The story is that when Gautam Buddha died he reached the doors of paradise. Those doors rarely open, only once in a while, in centuries—visitors don't come every day, and whenever someone comes to those doors the whole of paradise celebrates it. One more consciousness has attained to flowering, and existence is far richer than it has ever been before.

The doors were opened, and the other enlightened people who had entered into paradise before... because in Buddhism there is no God, but these enlightened people are godly—so there are as many gods as enlightened people. They had all gathered at the door with music, with song and with dance. They wanted to welcome Gautam Buddha but to their amazement he was standing with his back to the gate. His face was still looking toward the far shore that he had left behind.

They said, "This is strange. For whom are you waiting?"

He's reported to have said, "My heart is not so small. I'm waiting for all those I have left behind who are struggling on the way. They are my fellow travelers. You can keep the doors closed—you will have to wait a little for the celebration of my entering into paradise, because I have decided to enter this door as the last man. When everybody else has become enlightened and entered the door, when there is nobody left outside, then my time will have come to enter."

This story is a story—it cannot be an actual fact. It is not within your hands; once you have become enlightened you will have to enter into the universal source of life. It is not a question of your choice or decision. But the story is that he is still trying, even after his death. This story arose out of what he had said he was going to do on the last day before his death—that he would wait for you all.

He cannot wait here any longer, he has already waited over his time. He should have been gone by now but, seeing your misery and your suffering, he somehow kept himself together. But it has become more and more impossible. He will have to leave you—reluctantly—but he will wait for you on the other shore; he will not enter paradise, it is a promise: "So don't forget that for you, I will be standing there for centuries. But hurry, don't let me down, and don't let me wait too long."

Sincerity

Only one thing has to be remembered: be authentic, be sincere to yourself. Declare your truth, whatsoever the cost. Even if life is risked, risk it, because truth is far more valuable than anything, because truth is true life.

I am reminded of Bodhidharma, who introduced Zen into China… The emperor had come to receive him on the border—and if it had been somebody else in Bodhidharma's place, the emperor would have cut his head immediately, because he was behaving in such an unmannerly way. The emperor had created hundreds of temples, made thousands of Buddha statues. One thousand scholars were continuously translating Buddha's words from Pali into Chinese, and ten thousand Buddhist monks were fed by the imperial treasury. He had done much to make China Buddhist. Obviously, he thought that he would be appreciated, so he said, "I have done these things. What do you think—what will be the virtue attained out of all this?"

Sincerity

Bodhidharma's Search for a Disciple

Bodhidharma said, "Virtue? You idiot!"—in front of the whole court, because the court had come with the emperor. There was silence. He said, "You will go directly to hell!"

The emperor could not understand. He said, "I don't see why you are so angry."

Bodhidharma replied, "You are destroying a living word, and you are feeding these scholars who have nothing to contribute to the consciousness of the people. Still you have the nerve to ask if you are doing great virtue? You will suffer in hellfire!"

The emperor thought, "How to get out of this man's trap? I have entered in a lion's den and now it is very difficult to get out..." The emperor went back, and Bodhidharma remained in the hills just outside China's boundary. Sitting in a temple, facing the wall for nine years, he declared, "To talk to people who don't understand is just like talking to a wall. But talking to a wall at least one has a consolation that it is a wall. I will turn my face only when I see that somebody has come who is worthy of listening to the living word."

Nine years is a long time—but finally one morning the man came. He said, "Listen, I think I am the person you are waiting for." As a proof he cut off one of his hands with his sword, threw the hand into the lap of Bodhidharma and said, "Turn towards me; otherwise I will cut off my head and you will be responsible for it!"

Bodhidharma turned immediately. He said, "This is enough. This is enough proof that you are as crazy as I want! Sit down. There is no need to cut off your head —we have to use it; you are going to be my successor."

A man who cuts his hand just to give proof of his sincere search... and there was no doubt in Bodhidharma's mind that if he did not turn he would have cut his head. Unnecessarily, he would be burdened with the responsibility of killing a man, and such a beautiful man, so courageous. And certainly the man was Bodhidharma's successor.

But what happened between these two, nobody knows. Not a single word—Bodhidharma just turned towards him, told him to sit down, looked into his eyes... snow was falling and there was an immense silence all around. Not a single question was asked, and not a single answer was given. But something must have transpired, otherwise Bodhidharma would not have chosen him as his disciple.

Ultimate Accident

It is not a certain sequence of causes that brings enlightenment. Your search, your intense longing, your readiness to do anything—altogether perhaps they create a certain aroma around you in which that great accident becomes possible.

The nun Chiyono studied for years, but was unable to find enlightenment. One night, she was carrying an old pail filled with water. As she was walking along, she was watching the full moon reflected in the pail of water. Suddenly, the bamboo strips that held the pail together broke, and the pail fell apart. The water rushed out; the moon's reflection disappeared—and Chiyono became enlightened. She wrote this verse:

This way and that way I tried to keep the pail together, hoping the weak bamboo would never break. Suddenly the bottom fell out.

No more water; no more moon in the water—emptiness in my hand.

Ultimate Accident

Chiyono and her Bucket of Water

Enlightenment is always like an accident because it is unpredictable—because you cannot manage it, you cannot cause it to happen. But don't misunderstand me, because when I say enlightenment is just like an accident, I am not saying don't do anything to attain it. The accident happens only to those who have been doing much for it—but it never happens because of their doing. The doing is just a cause which creates the situation in them so they become accident-prone, that's all. That is the meaning of this beautiful happening.

I must tell you something about Chiyono. She was a very beautiful woman—when she was young, even the emperor and the princes were after her. She refused because she wanted to be a lover only to the divine. She went from one monastery to another to become a nun; but even great masters refused—there were so many monks, and she was so beautiful that they would forget God and everything. So everywhere the door was closed.

So what did Chiyono do? Finding no other way, she burned her face, scarred her whole face. And then she went to a master; he couldn't even recognize whether she was a woman or a man. Then she was accepted as a nun. She studied, meditated for thirty, forty years continuously. Then suddenly, one night… she was looking at the moon reflected in the pail. Suddenly the pail fell down, the water rushed out, and the moon disappeared—and that became the trigger-point.

There is always a trigger-point from where the old disappears and the new starts, from where you are reborn. That became the trigger-point. Suddenly, the water rushed out and there was no moon. So she must have looked up—and the real moon was there. Suddenly she became awakened to this fact, that everything was a reflection, an illusion, because it was seen through the mind. As the pail broke, the mind inside also broke. It was ready. All that could be done had been done. All that could be possible, she had done it. Nothing was left, she was ready, she had earned it. This ordinary incident became a trigger-point.

Suddenly the bottom fell out—it was an accident. *No more water; no more moon in the water— emptiness in my hand.*

And this is enlightenment: when emptiness is in your hand, when everything is empty, when there is nobody, not even you. You have attained to the original face of Zen.

GREED

Whenever people become very greedy they become very hurried, and go on finding more ways to gain more speed. They are continuously on the run because they think that life is running out. These are the people who say, "Time is money." Time is money? Money is very limited; time is unlimited. Time is not money, time is eternity—it has always been there and will always be there. And you have always been here and you will always be here.

So drop greed, and don't be bothered about the result. Sometimes it happens that because of your impatience, you miss many things.

Greed/Beyond Greed

A Parable of Ambition and Hurry

I will tell you an ancient Hindu parable....

A great saint, Narada, was going to paradise. He used to travel between paradise and earth. He functioned like a postman between that world and this world; he was a bridge.

He came across an ancient sage, very old, sitting under a tree and repeating his mantra. He had been repeating that mantra for many years and many lives. Narada asked him, "Would you like to ask about something? Would you like some message to be given to the Lord?" The old man opened his eyes and said, "Just you inquire about one thing: how much longer do I have to wait? How long? Tell him it is too much. For many lives I have been doing this mantra, now how long am I expected to do it? I am tired of it. I am bored with it."

Just by the side of the ancient sage underneath another tree was a young man with an ektara, a one-stringed instrument, playing it and dancing. Narada asked him jokingly, "Would you also like to inquire about how long it will take for your enlightenment to happen?" But the young man did not even bother to answer. He continued his dance. Narada asked again, "I am going to the Lord. Have you some message?" But the young man laughed and continued to dance.

When Narada came back after a few days he told the old man, "God said that you will have to wait at least three lives more." The old man became so angry that he threw down his beads. He was almost ready to hit Narada! And he said, "This is nonsense! I have been waiting and waiting and I have been doing all kinds of austerities—chanting, fasting, all forms of rituals. I have fulfilled all the requirements. Three lives—this is unjust!"

The young man was still dancing under his tree, very joyously. Narada was afraid, but still he went and told him, "Although you did not ask, out of my own curiosity I inquired. When God said that that old man would have to wait three lives, I inquired about the young man nearby, dancing and playing his ektara. And he said, 'That young man—he will have to wait as many lives as there are leaves on the tree under which he is dancing.'"

And the young man started dancing even faster and he said, "Just as many leaves as are on this tree? then it is not very far, then I have already arrived!—just think how many trees there are on the whole earth. Compare! So it is very close. Thank you, sir, that you inquired." He started dancing again. And the story says that the young man became instantly enlightened, that very moment.

Beyond Greed

Greed/Beyond Greed

Man is full if he is in tune with the universe; if he is not in tune with the universe then he is empty, utterly empty. And out of that emptiness comes greed. Greed is to fill it—with money, with houses, with furniture, with friends, with lovers, with anything—because one cannot live as emptiness. It is horrifying, it is a ghost life. If you are empty and there is nothing inside you, it is impossible to live.

To have the feeling that you have much inside you, there are only two ways: either you get in tune with the universe... Then you are filled with the whole, with all the flowers and with all the stars. They are within you just as they are without you. That is real fulfillment. But if you don't do that—and millions of people are not doing that—then the easiest way is to fill it with any junk.

Greed simply means you are feeling a deep emptiness and you want to fill it with anything possible, it doesn't matter what it is. And once you understand it, then you have nothing to do with greed. You have something to do with coming into communion with the whole, so the inner emptiness disappears. And with it, all greed disappears.

But there are mad people all over the world, and they are collecting things to fill their emptiness. Somebody is collecting money although he never uses it. People are eating; they are not feeling hungry and still they go on swallowing. They know that this is going to create suffering, they will be sick, but they cannot prevent themselves. This eating is also a filling-up process. So there can be many ways to fill emptiness, although it is never full—it remains empty, and you remain miserable because it is never enough. More is needed, and the more and the demand for more is unending.

You have to understand the emptiness that you are trying to fill, and ask the question, "Why am I empty? The whole existence is so full, why am I empty? Perhaps I have lost track—I am no longer moving in the same direction, I am no longer existential. That is the cause of my emptiness."

So be existential.

Let go, and move closer to existence in silence and peace, in meditation.

And one day you will see you are so full—overfull, overflowing—of joy, of blissfulness, of benediction. You have so much of it that you can give it to the whole world and yet it will not be exhausted.

That day, for the first time you will not feel any greed—for money, for food, for things, for anything. You will live naturally, and whatever is needed you will find it.

Disciplehood

No situation is without a lesson, no situation at all. All situations are pregnant, but you have to discover; it may not be available on the surface. You have to be watchful, you have to look at all the aspects of the situation.

Disciplehood

The Many Teachers of Junnaid

One of the great Sufi Masters, Junnaid, was asked when he was dying... his chief disciple came close to him and asked, "Master, you are leaving us. One question has always been in our minds but we could never gather courage enough to ask you. Who was your Master? This has been a great curiosity among your disciples because we have never heard you talk about your Master."

Junnaid opened his eyes and said, "It will be very difficult for me to answer because I have learned from almost everybody. The whole existence has been my Master. I have learned from every event that has happened in my life. And I am grateful to all that has happened, because out of all that learning I have arrived."

Junnaid said, "Just to satisfy your curiosity I will give you three instances. One: I was very thirsty and I was going towards the river carrying my begging bowl, the only possession I had. When I reached the river a dog rushed, jumped into the river, started drinking.

"I watched for a moment and threw away my begging bowl—because it is useless. A dog can do without it. I also jumped into the river, drank as much water as I wanted. My whole body was cool because I had jumped into the river. I sat in the river for a few moments, thanked the dog, touched his feet with deep reverence because he had taught me a lesson. I had dropped everything, all possessions, but there was a certain clinging to my begging bowl. It was a beautiful bowl, very beautifully carved, and I was always aware that somebody might steal it. Even in the night I used to put it under my head as a pillow so nobody could snatch it away. That was my last clinging—the dog helped. It was so clear: if a dog can manage without a begging bowl… I am a man, why can't I manage? That dog was one of my Masters.

"Secondly," he said, "I lost my way in a forest and by the time I reached the nearest village that I could find, it was midnight. Everybody was fast asleep. I wandered all over the town to see if I could find somebody awake to give me shelter for the night, until finally I found one man. I asked him, 'It seems only two persons are awake in the town, you and I. Can you give me shelter for the night?'

"The man said, 'I can see from your gown that you are a Sufi monk....'"

The word *Sufi* comes from *suf*; *suf* means wool, a woolen garment. The Sufis have used the woolen garment for centuries; hence they are called Sufis because of their garment. The thief said, "I can see you are a Sufi and I feel a little embarrassed to take you to my home. I am perfectly willing, but I must tell you who I am. I am a thief—would you like to be a guest of a thief?"

For a moment Junnaid hesitated. The thief said, "Look, it is better I told you. You seem hesitant. The thief is willing but the mystic seems to be hesitant to enter into the house of a thief, as if the mystic is weaker than the thief. In fact, I should be afraid of you—you may change me, you may transform my whole life! Inviting you means danger, but I am not afraid. You are welcome. Come to my home. Eat, drink, go to sleep, and stay as long as you want, because I live alone and my earning is enough. I can manage for two persons. And it will be really beautiful to chit-chat with you of great things. But you seem to be hesitant."

And Junnaid became aware that it was true. He asked to be forgiven. He touched the feet of the thief and he said, "Yes, my rootedness in my own being is yet very weak. You are really a strong man and I would like to come to your home. And I would like to stay a little longer, not only for this night. I want to be stronger myself!"

The thief said, "Come on!" He fed the Sufi, gave him something to drink, helped him to prepare for sleep and he said, "Now I will go. I have to do my own thing. I will come back early in the morning."

Early in the morning the thief came back. Junnaid asked, "Have you been successful?"

The thief said, "No, not today, but I will see tomorrow."

And this happened continuously, for thirty days: every night the thief went out, and every morning he came back empty-handed. But he was never sad, never frustrated—no sign of failure on his face, always happy —and he would say, "It doesn't matter. I tried my best. I could not find anything today again, but tomorrow I will try. And, God willing, it can happen tomorrow if it has not happened today."

After one month Junnaid left, and for years he tried to realize the ultimate, and it was always a failure. But each time he decided to drop the whole project he remembered the thief, his smiling face and his saying "God willing, what has not happened today may happen tomorrow."

Junnaid said, "I remembered the thief as one of my greatest Masters. Without him I would not be what I am.

"And third," he said, "I entered into a small village. A little boy was carrying a lit candle, obviously going to the small temple of the town to put the candle there for the night."

And Junnaid asked, "Can you tell me from where the light comes? You have lighted the candle yourself so

Disciplehood

you must have seen. What is the source of light?"

The boy laughed and he said, "Wait!" And he blew out the candle in front of Junnaid. And he said, "You have seen the light go. Can you tell me where it has gone? If you can tell me where it has gone I will tell you from where it has come, because it has gone to the same place. It has returned to the source."

And Junnaid said, "I had met great philosophers but nobody had made such a beautiful statement: 'It has gone to its very source.' Everything returns to its source finally. Moreover, the child made me aware of my own ignorance. I was trying to joke with the child, but the joke was on me. He showed me that asking foolish questions—'From where has the light come?'—is not intelligent. It comes from nowhere, from nothingness—and it goes back to nowhere, to nothingness."

Junnaid said, "I touched the feet of the child. The child was puzzled. He said, 'Why you are touching my feet?' And I told him, 'You are my Master—you have shown me something. You have given me a great lesson, a great insight.'

"Since that time," Junnaid said, "I have been meditating on nothingness and slowly, slowly I have entered into nothingness. And now the final moment has come when the candle will go out, the light will go out. And I know where I am going—to the same source.

"I remember that child with gratefulness. I can still see him standing before me blowing out the candle."

The Greatest Miracle

To do a miracle is great, but not great enough. To do a miracle is still to be in the world of the ego. A real greatness is so ordinary that it claims nothing; it is so ordinary that it never tries to prove anything.

The Greatest Miracle

On the Temptations of Spiritual Powers

A man came to Lin Chi and said, "My master is a great psychic. What do you say about your Master? What can your Master do, what miracles?"

Lin Chi asked, "What miracles has your Master been doing?"

The disciple said, "One day he told me to go to the other bank of the river, and I stood there with a piece of paper in my hand. The river was very wide, almost one mile. He was standing on the other bank and from there he started writing with a fountain pen, and the writing came on my paper. This I have seen myself, I am a witness! What can your Master do?"

Lin Chi said, "When he is hungry he eats, and when he is sleepy he goes to sleep."

The man said, "What are you talking about? You call these miracles? Everybody is doing that!"

Lin Chi said, "Nobody is doing that. When you sleep you do a thousand and one things. When you eat you think a thousand and one things. When my Master sleeps he simply sleeps; no tossing, no turning, not even a dream. Only sleep exists in that moment, nothing else. And when he feels hungry he eats. He is always wherever he is."

What is the point of writing from one bank of a river to the other bank? It is just foolish. Only foolish people would be interested in it. What is the point?

Somebody went to Ramakrishna and said, "My Master is a great man. He can walk on the water."

Ramakrishna said, "Foolish! Because I can simply go to the ferryman, and for just two pennies he takes me to the other side. Your Master is a fool. Go and make him aware that he should not waste his life. It can be done so easily."

But the mind is always hankering. The mind is nothing but hankering, desiring something to happen. Sometimes it is thinking about money, to have more money, to have bigger houses, to have more respectability, to have more political power. Then you turn towards spirituality; the mind remains the same. Now you want to have more psychic powers—telepathy, clairvoyance, and all sorts of nonsense. But the mind remains the same—you want more. The same game continues....

Now it is telepathy, or clairvoyance, or psychic powers: "If you can do this, I can do more than this. I can read people's thoughts thousands of miles away."

Life in itself is a miracle, but the ego is not ready to accept that. It wants to do something special, something that nobody else is doing, something extraordinary.

WORTH

Don't be bothered too much about utilitarian ends. Rather, constantly remember that you are not here in life to become a commodity. You are not here to become a utility—that is below dignity. You are not here just to become more and more efficient—you are here to become more and more alive; you are here to become more and more intelligent; you are here to become more and more happy, ecstatically happy.

Worth

On the Virtues of Uselessness

Lao Tzu was traveling with his disciples and they came to a forest where hundreds of carpenters were cutting trees, because a great palace was being built. Almost the whole forest had been cut, but one tree was standing there, a big tree with thousands of branches—so big that ten thousand persons could sit under its shade. Lao Tzu asked his disciples to go and inquire why this tree had not been cut yet, when the whole forest had been cut and was deserted.

The disciples went and they asked the carpenters, "Why have you not cut this tree?"

The carpenters said, "This tree is absolutely useless. You cannot make anything out of it because every branch has so many knots in it. Nothing is straight. You cannot make pillars out of it, you cannot make furniture out of it. You cannot use it as fuel because the smoke is so dangerous to the eyes—you almost go blind. This tree is absolutely useless. That's why."

They came back. Lao Tzu laughed and he said, "Be like this tree. If you want to survive in this world be like this tree—absolutely useless. Then nobody will harm you. If you are straight you will be cut, you will become furniture in somebody's house. If you are beautiful you will be sold in the market, you will become a commodity. Be like this tree, absolutely useless. Then nobody can harm you. And you will grow big and vast, and thousands of people can find shade under you."

Lao Tzu has a logic altogether different from your mind. He says: Be the last. Move in the world as if you are not. Remain unknown. Don't try to be the first, don't be competitive, don't try to prove your worth. There is no need. Remain useless and enjoy.

Of course he is impractical. But if you understand him you will find that he is the most practical on a deeper layer, in the depth—because life is to enjoy and celebrate, life is not to become a utility. Life is more like poetry than like a commodity in the market; it should be like poetry, a song, a dance.

Lao Tzu says: If you try to be very clever, if you try to be very useful, you will be used. If you try to be very practical, somewhere or other you will be harnessed, because the world cannot leave the practical man alone. Lao Tzu says: Drop all these ideas. If you want to be a poem, an ecstasy, then forget about utility. Remain true to yourself.

Recognition

The longing of the mind is to be extraordinary. The ego thirsts and hungers for the recognition that you are somebody. Somebody achieves that dream through wealth, somebody else achieves that dream through power, politics; somebody else can achieve that dream through miracles, jugglery, but the dream remains the same: "I cannot tolerate being nobody."

And this is a miracle— when you accept your nobodiness, when you are just as ordinary as anybody else, when you don't ask for any recognition, when you can exist as if you are not existing. To be absent is the miracle.

This story is beautiful, one of the most beautiful Zen anecdotes, and Bankei is one of the superb Masters. But Bankei was an ordinary man.

Once it happened that Bankei was working in his garden. A seeker came, a man in search of a Master, and he asked Bankei, "Gardener, where is the Master?"

Bankei laughed and said, "Wait. Go in through that door, and inside you will find the Master."

Recognition

The Master, the Gardener, and the Guest

So the man went round and came inside. He saw Bankei sitting on a throne, the same man who was the gardener outside. The seeker said, "Are you kidding? Get down from this throne. This is sacrilegious, you don't pay any respect to the Master."

Bankei got down, sat on the ground, and said, "Now then, it is difficult. Now you will not find the master here … because I am the Master."

It was difficult for that man to see that a great Master could work in the garden, could be just ordinary. He left. He couldn't believe that this man was the Master; he missed.

Everybody is afraid of being nobody. Only very rare and extraordinary people are not afraid of being nobody —a Gautam Buddha, a Bankei. A nobody is not an ordinary phenomenon; it is one of the greatest experiences in life—that you are, and still you are not. That you are just pure existence with no name, with no address, with no boundaries... neither a sinner nor a saint, neither inferior nor superior, just a silence.

People are afraid because their whole personality will be gone; their name, their fame, their respectability, all will be gone; hence, the fear. But death is going to take them away from you anyway. Those who are wise allow these things to drop by themselves. Then nothing is left for death to take away. Then all fear disappears, because death cannot come to you; you don't have anything for death. Death cannot kill a nobody.

Once you feel your nobodiness you have become immortal. The experience of nobodiness is exactly the meaning of nirvana, of nothingness, of absolute undisturbed silence, with no ego, with no personality, with no hypocrisy—just this silence... and these insects singing in the night.

You are here in a way, and still you are not.

You are here because of the old association with the body, but look within and you are not. And this insight, where there is pure silence and pure isness, is your reality, which death cannot destroy. This is your eternity, this is your immortality.

There is nothing to fear. There is nothing to lose. And if you think anything is lost—your name, your respectability, your fame—they are worthless. They are playthings for children, not for mature people. It is time for you to be mature, it is time for you to be ripe, time for you just to be.

Your somebodiness is so small. The more you are somebody, the smaller you are; the more you are nobody, the bigger. Be absolutely nobody, and you are one with the existence itself.

Questioning

One who goes into questions strays off into the jungle of philosophy. Let questions come and go. Look at the crowd of questions like you look at people moving on the street—nothing to give, nothing to take—with detachment, standing far away... The more distance there is between you and your questions, the better. Because it is in this gap the answer will arise.

Questioning

The Professor and his Thirst for Answers

A professor of philosophy went to a Zen Master, Nan-in, and he asked about God, about nirvana, about meditation, and so many things. The Master listened silently—questions and questions and questions—and then he said, "You look tired. You have climbed this high mountain; you have come from a faraway place. Let me first serve you tea." And the Zen Master made tea. The professor waited—he was boiling with questions. And when the Master was making tea and the samovar was singing and the aroma of the tea started spreading, the Master said to the professor, "Wait, don't be in such a hurry. Who knows? Even by drinking tea your questions may be answered... or even before that."

The professor was at a loss. He started thinking, "This whole journey has been a wastage. This man seems to be mad. How can my question about God be answered by drinking tea? What relevance is there? It is better to escape from here as soon as possible." But he was also feeling tired and it was good to have a cup of tea before he started descending back down the mountain.

The Master brought the kettle, poured tea in the cup—and went on pouring. The cup was full, and the tea started overflowing into the saucer, but he went on pouring. Then the saucer was also full. Just one drop more and the tea would start flowing on the floor, and the professor said, "Stop! What are you doing? Are you mad or something? Can't you see the cup is full? Can't you see the saucer is full?"

And the Zen Master said, "That's the exact situation you are in: your mind is so full of questions that even if I answer, you don't have any space for the answer to go in. But you look like an intelligent man. You could see the point, that now even a single drop more of tea and it will not be contained by the cup or the saucer, it will start overflowing on the floor. And I tell you, since you entered this house your questions are overflowing all over the place. This small but is full of your questions! Go back, empty your cup, and then come. First create a little space in yourself."

Dropping Knowledge

Truth is your own experience, your own vision. Even if I have seen the truth and I tell you, the moment I tell you it will become a lie for you, not a truth. For me it was truth, for me it came through the eyes. It was my vision. For you, it will not be your vision, it will be a borrowed thing. It will be a belief, it will be knowledge—not knowing. And if you start believing in it, you will be believing a lie. Now remember it. Even a truth becomes a lie if it enters your being through the wrong door. The truth has to enter through the front door, through the eyes. Truth is a vision. One has to see it.

Naropa was a great scholar, a great pundit, with ten thousand disciples of his own. One day he was sitting surrounded by thousands of scriptures—ancient, very ancient, rare. Suddenly he fell asleep, must have been tired, and he saw a vision.

He saw a very, very old, ugly, horrible woman—a hag. Her ugliness was such that he started trembling in his sleep. It was so nauseating he wanted to escape—but where to escape, where to go? He was caught, as if hypnotized by the old hag. Her eyes were like magnets.

Dropping Knowledge

Naropa's Haunting Vision

"What are you studying?" asked the old woman.

He said, "Philosophy, religion, epistemology, language, grammar, logic."

The old woman asked again, "Do you understand them?"

Naropa said, "Of course... Yes, I understand them."

The woman asked again, "Do you understand the word, or the sense?"

Thousands of questions had been asked to Naropa in his life—thousands of students always asking, inquiring—but nobody had asked this: whether he understands the word, or the sense. And the woman's eyes were so penetrating—those eyes were going to the very depth of his being, and it was impossible to lie. To anybody else he would have said, "Of course I understand the sense," but to this woman, this horrible-looking woman, he had to say the truth. He said, "I understand the words."

The woman was very happy. She started dancing and laughing, and her ugliness was transformed; a subtle beauty started coming out of her being. Thinking, "I have made her so happy. Why not make her a little more happy?" Naropa then said, "And yes, I understand the sense also."

The woman stopped laughing, stopped dancing. She started crying and weeping and all her ugliness was back—a thousandfold more. Naropa said, "Why are you weeping and crying? And why were you laughing and dancing before?"

The woman said, "I was happy because a great scholar like you didn't lie. But now I am crying and weeping because you have lied to me. I know—and you know—that you don't understand the sense."

The vision disappeared and Naropa was transformed. He escaped from the university, he never again touched a scripture in his life. He became completely ignorant, he understood—the woman was nobody outside, it was just a projection. It was Naropa's own being, through knowledge, that had became ugly. Just this much understanding, that "I don't understand the sense," and the ugliness was transformed immediately into a beautiful phenomenon.

This vision of Naropa is very significant. Unless you feel that knowledge is useless you will never be in search of wisdom. You will carry the false coin thinking that this is the real treasure. You have to become aware that knowledge is a false coin—it is not knowing, it is not understanding. At the most it is intellectual—the word has been understood but the sense lost.

AUTHENTICITY

The real thing is not a path. The real thing is the authenticity of the seeker. Let me emphasize this.

You can travel on any path. If you are sincere and authentic, you will reach the goal. Some paths may be hard, some may be easier, some may have greenery on both sides, some may be moving through deserts, some may have beautiful scenery around them, some may not have any scenery around them, that's another thing; but if you are sincere and honest and authentic and true, then each path leads to the goal.

So it simply can be reduced to one thing: that authenticity is the path. No matter what path you follow, if you are authentic, every path leads to the goal. And the opposite is also true: no matter what path you follow, if you are not authentic you will not reach anywhere. Your authenticity brings you back home, nothing else. All paths are secondary. The basic thing is to be authentic, to be true.

AUTHENTICITY

MILAREPA AND THE FALSE TEACHER

It is reported about one great mystic, Milarepa:

When he went to his master in Tibet he was so humble, so pure, so authentic, that other disciples became jealous of him. It was certain that he would be the successor. And of course there was politics, so they tried to kill him.

One day they said to him, "If you really believe in the master, can you jump from the hill? If you really believe, if the trust is there, then nothing, no harm, is going to happen." And Milarepa jumped without even hesitating for a single moment. They rushed down… because it was almost a three-thousand-foot deep valley. They went down to find his scattered bones—but he was sitting there in a lotus posture, very happy, tremendously happy. He opened his eyes and said, "You are right, trust protects."

They thought it must be some coincidence, so when a house was on fire one day they told him, "If you love your master and you trust, you can go in." He rushed in to save the woman and the child who were left inside. He rushed in, and the fire was so great that the other disciples were hoping that he would die—but when he came back out with the woman and child, he was not burned at all. And he became more and more radiant, because the trust....

One day they were going somewhere, they were to cross a river, and they told him, "You need not go in the boat. You have such great trust, you can walk on the river"—and he walked.

That was the first time the master saw him. He was not aware that Milarepa had been told to jump into the valley and told to go into the burning house. But that time he was there on the bank and he saw Milarepa walking on the water and he said, "What are you doing? It is impossible!"

And Milarepa said, "Not impossible at all! I am doing it by your power, sir."

Now the Master thought, "If my name and my power can do this to this ignorant, stupid man.... I have never tried it myself,"...so he tried. He drowned. Nothing has been heard about him after that.

Alertness

Be alert. Each moment has to be taken as if this were the last moment. And there is every possibility this may be the last moment! So use it totally. Squeeze the juices out of it totally. In that very totality you will be alert.

Alertness

The Sudden Death of Ekido's Disciple

The Japanese master Ekido was a severe teacher and his pupils feared him.

One day, while striking the time of day on the temple gong, one of his pupils missed a beat because he was watching a beautiful girl who was passing the gates.

Unknown to the pupil, Ekido was standing behind him. Ekido struck the pupil with his staff, and the shock stopped the heart of the pupil, and he died.

Look at this story and you may think that the Master killed his disciple. That is not the thing. The disciple was going to die anyhow; it was the moment for his death. The Master knew it; he simply used the moment of death for the disciple's enlightenment. This is not said in the story, but this is how the thing happened; otherwise why was the Master standing behind him? Had he not anything more significant to do? But at that moment there was nothing more significant, because this disciple was going to die and this death had to be used.

The story is beautiful and very significant. The disciple saw a beautiful girl passing and his whole consciousness was lost. His whole being became a desire—he wanted to follow this girl, to possess this girl. He was alert just a moment before, now he was not alert.

He was beating the gong fully alert. This is part of meditation in a Zen monastery—whatsoever you do, do it with awareness. Whatsoever you do, be there in it as a light, and everything is revealed. So this disciple at the moment of death was going to be alert and aware, and the mind did the last thing, its final resort—a beautiful girl appeared!

At this moment, when the disciple missed awareness, the Master hit him hard on the head. The Master is seeing the invisible death reaching, and he hits just to make the disciple alert. The Master was waiting behind. Masters are always waiting behind disciples, whether physically or non-physically—and this is one of the greatest moments, when a person is going to die. The Master hit him hard, his body fell down, but inside he became alert. The desire disappeared. Everything dropped with the body, shattered; he became alert. In that alertness, he died. And if you can join alertness and death you have become enlightened.

Imitation

Be true to yourself, because your own truth can lead you to the ultimate truth. Nobody else's truth can be your truth.

You have a seed within you. Only if that seed sprouts and becomes a tree will you have a flowering; then you will have an ecstasy, a benediction. But if you are following others that seed will remain dead. And you may accumulate all the ideals in the world and become successful, but you will feel empty, because nothing else can fill you—only your seed, when it becomes a tree, will fill you. You will feel fulfillment only when your truth has come to flower, never before.

Imitation

Gutei's Finger Pointing to the One

The Zen master Gutei made a practice of raising his finger whenever he explained a question about Zen.

A very young disciple began to imitate him, and whenever anyone asked the disciple what his master had been preaching about, the boy would raise his finger.

Gutei got to hear about this, and when he came upon the boy as he was doing it one day, he seized the boy, whipped out a knife, cut off his finger, and threw it away.

As the boy ran off howling Gutei shouted, "Stop!"

The boy stopped, turned round, and looked at his master through his tears. Gutei was holding up his own finger.

The boy went to hold up his finger, and when he realized it wasn't there he bowed.

In that instant he became enlightened.

This is a very strange story, and there is every possibility that you will misunderstand it, because the most difficult thing to understand in life is the behavior of an enlightened person.

Masters never do anything unnecessarily, not even raising a finger… Gutei didn't always raise a finger, only when he explained a question about Zen—why? All your problems arise because you are fragmented, because you are a disunity, a chaos, not a harmony. And what is meditation? Nothing but coming to a unity. Gutei's explanations were secondary; the one raised finger was the primary thing. He was saying, "Be one! and all your problems will be solved."

The boy began to imitate him. Now, imitation cannot lead you anywhere. Imitation means that the ideal comes from without, it is not something happening within you. You have a seed within you; if you are imitating others that seed will remain dead.

Gutei must have been very, very compassionate. Only out of compassion you can be so hard—the imitation has to be cut severely. The finger is just symbolic. The boy has to be shocked severely, and the suffering must go to the very root of his being. A very intense moment of awareness, a very great device… Gutei shouted, "Stop!" In the moment of stopping there was no more pain.

Just out of old habit, when the master raises his finger the boy raises his—which is not there. And for the first time he realizes that he is not the body—he is awareness, consciousness. He is a soul, and the body is just the house.

You are the light within—not the lamp, but the flame.

A Cup of Tea

Awareness comes through sensitivity. You have to be more sensitive whatsoever you do, so that even a trivial thing like tea... Can you find anything more trivial than tea? Can you find anything more ordinary than tea? No, you cannot—and Zen monks and masters have raised this most ordinary thing into the most extraordinary. They have bridged "this" and "that"... as if tea and God have become one. Unless tea becomes divine you will not be divine, because the least has to be raised to the most, the ordinary has to be raised to the extraordinary, the earth has to be made heaven. They have to be bridged, no gap should be left.

A Cup of Tea

Bodhidharma's Eyelids and the Origins of Tea

Tea was discovered by Bodhidharma, the founder of Zen. The story is beautiful.

He was meditating for nine years, facing a wall. Nine years, just facing the wall, continuously, and sometimes it was natural that he might start falling asleep. He fought and fought with his sleep—remember, the metaphysical sleep, the unconsciousness. He wanted to remain conscious even while asleep. He wanted to make a continuity of consciousness—the light should go on burning day and night, for twenty-four hours. That's what *dhyana* is, what meditation is—awareness.

One night he felt that it was impossible to keep awake; he was falling asleep. He cut his eyelids off and threw them! Now there was no way for him to close his eyes. The story is beautiful.

To get to the inner eyes, these outer eyes will have to be thrown. That much price has to be paid.

And what happened? After a few days he found that those eyelids that he had thrown on the ground had started growing into a small sprout. That sprout became tea. That's why when you drink tea, something of Bodhidharma enters you and you cannot fall asleep. Bodhidharma was meditating on the mountain called T'a, that's why it is called tea. It comes from that mountain where Bodhidharma meditated for nine years. This is a parable.

When the Zen Master says, "Have a cup of tea," he's saying, "Taste a little of Bodhidharma. Don't bother about these questions, whether God exists or not, who created the world, where is heaven and where is hell and what is the theory of karma and rebirth." When the Zen Master says, "Forget all about it. Have a cup of tea," he's saying, "Better become more aware, don't go into all this nonsense. This is not going to help you at all."

Meditation

Do the small things of life with a relaxed awareness. When you are eating, eat totally—chew totally, taste totally, smell totally. Touch your bread, feel the texture. Smell the bread, smell the flavor. Chew it, let it dissolve into your being, and remain conscious—and you are meditating. And then meditation is not separate from life.

Whenever meditation is separate from life, something is wrong. It becomes life-negative. Then one starts thinking of going to a monastery or to a Himalayan cave. Then one wants to escape from life, because life seems to be a distraction from meditation.

Life is not a distraction, life is an occasion for meditation.

Meditation

On which side of your umbrella did you leave your shoes?

A disciple had come to see Ikkyu, his master. The disciple had been practicing for some time. It was raining, and as he went in, he left his shoes and umbrella outside. After he paid his respects, the master asked him on which side of his shoes he had left his umbrella.

Now, what kind of question...? You don't expect masters to ask such nonsense questions—you expect them to ask about God, about kundalini rising, chakras opening, lights happening in your head. You ask about such great things—occult, esoteric. But Ikkyu asked a very ordinary question. No Christian saint would have asked it, no Jain monk would have asked it, no Hindu swami would have asked it. It can be done only by one who is really with the Buddha, in the Buddha—who is really a buddha himself. The master asked him on which side of his shoes he had left his umbrella. Now, what do shoes and umbrellas have to do with spirituality?

If the same question had been asked to you, you would have felt annoyed. What kind of question is this?

But there is something immensely valuable in it. Had he asked about God, about your kundalini and chakras, that would have been nonsense, utterly meaningless. But this has meaning. The disciple could not remember—who bothers where you have put your shoes and on which side you have put your umbrella, to the right or to the left. Who bothers? Who pays so much attention to umbrellas? Who thinks of shoes? Who is so careful?

But that was enough—the disciple was refused. Ikkyu said, "Then go and meditate for seven years more."

"Seven years?" the disciple said. "Just for this small fault?"

Ikkyu said, "This is not a small fault. Faults are not small or big—you are just not yet living meditatively, that's all. Go back, meditate for seven years more, and come again."

This is the essential message: Be careful, careful of everything. And don't make any distinction between things, that this is trivia and that is spiritual. It depends on you. Pay attention, be careful, and everything becomes spiritual. Don't pay attention, don't be careful, and everything becomes unspiritual.

Spirituality is imparted by you, it is your gift to the world. When a master like Ikkyu touches his umbrella, the umbrella is as divine as anything can be. Meditative energy is alchemical. It transforms the base metal into gold; it goes on transforming the baser into the higher. At the ultimate peak, everything is divine. This very world is the paradise, and this very body the buddha.

Remaining Centered

Wherever you are, become more centered, become more alert, live more consciously. There is nowhere else to go. Everything that has to happen, has to happen within you, and it is in your hands. You are not a puppet, and your strings are not in anybody else's hands. You are an absolutely free individual. If you decide to remain in illusions, you can remain so for many, many lives. If you decide to get out, a single moment's decision is enough.

You can be out of all illusions this very moment.

Buddha was staying in Vaishali, where Amrapali lived—Amrapali was a prostitute. In Buddha's time, in India, it was a convention that the most beautiful woman of any city will not be allowed to get married to any one person, because that will create unnecessary jealousy, conflict, fighting. So the most beautiful woman had to become *nagarvadhu*—the wife of the whole town.

Remaining Centered

The Monk and the Prostitute

It was not disreputable at all; on the contrary, they were very much respected. They were not ordinary prostitutes. They were only visited by the very rich, or the kings, or the princes, generals—the highest strata of society.

Amrapali was very beautiful. One day she was standing on her terrace and she saw a young Buddhist monk. She had never fallen in love with anybody, but she fell suddenly in love—a young man, but of a tremendous presence, awareness, grace. The way he was walking... She rushed down, she asked him, "After three days the rainy season is going to start..." Buddhist monks don't move for four months when it is the rainy season. Amrapali said, "I invite you to stay in my house for the four months."

The young monk said, "I will ask my master. If he allows me, I will come."

The young monk came, touched the feet of Buddha and told the whole story, "She has asked me to stay for four months in her house. I have told her that I will ask my master, so I am here... whatever you say."

Buddha looked into his eyes and said, "You can stay."

It was a shock. Ten thousand monks... There was great silence but great anger, great jealousy. After the young man left to stay with Amrapali, the monks every day started bringing gossips, "The whole city is agog. There is only one talk—that a Buddhist monk is staying with Amrapali."

Buddha said, "You should keep silent. I trust my monk. I have looked into his eyes—there was no desire. If I had said no, he would not have felt anything. I said yes... he simply went. And I trust in his awareness, in his meditation. Why are you getting so agitated and worried?"

After four months the young man came, touched Buddha's feet—and following him was Amrapali, dressed as a Buddhist nun. She touched Buddha's feet and she said, "I tried my best to seduce your monk, but he seduced me. He convinced me by his presence and awareness that the real life is at your feet."

And Buddha said to the assembly, "Now, are you satisfied or not?"

If meditation is deep, if awareness is clear, nothing can disturb it. And Amrapali became one of the enlightened women among Buddha's disciples.

Ego

Ego is a social phenomenon—it is society, it is not you. But it gives you a function in the society, a place in the hierarchy of the society. And if you remain satisfied with it, you will miss the whole opportunity of finding the real self. Have you ever noticed that all types of miseries enter through the ego? It cannot make you blissful; it can only make you miserable. Ego is hell. Whenever you suffer, just try to watch and analyze, and you will find, somewhere the ego is the cause of it.

20

EGO

THE WOMAN AND THE RIVER CROSSING

Two Buddhist monks are returning to their monastery; they come to a ford. The current is very powerful, it is a hilly place. A young, beautiful girl is waiting there, waiting for somebody to help her to cross. She is afraid to enter alone.

One monk, who is the older one of course... because he is older, he walks ahead—all games of the ego. If you are older, you have to walk ahead; younger monks have to walk a little back. The older monk comes first. The young girl asks him, "Would you help me; just hold my hand? I am afraid, the current is so strong and perhaps it may be deep."

The old man closes his eyes—that's what Buddha had said to the monks, that if you see a woman, particularly if she is beautiful, close your eyes. But I am surprised: you have already seen her, then you close your eyes; otherwise how can you determine she is a woman, and beautiful? You are already affected, and now you close your eyes! So he closes his eyes and enters the ford without answering the woman.

Then the second, younger monk comes. The girl is afraid, but there is nothing else to do—the sun is setting, soon it will be night. So she asks the young monk, "Will you please hold my hand? The ford seems to be deep and the current strong... and I am afraid."

The monk says, "It is deep, I know, and just holding hands won't do; you sit on my shoulders and I will carry you to the other side."

When they reach the monastery the older monk says to the young one, "You, fellow, you have committed a sin and I am going to report that not only you touched a woman, not only you talked with her, you carried her on your shoulders! You should be expelled from the community; you are not worthy of being a monk."

The young man simply laughs and says, "It seems although I have dropped that girl three miles back, you are still carrying her on your shoulders. Three miles have passed, and you are still bothered by it?"

Now, what is happening to this old monk? The girl was beautiful; he has missed a chance. He is angry, he is jealous. He is full of sexuality, he is really in a mess. The younger one is completely clean. He took the girl across and left her on the other shore, and that's that, the thing is finished.

Never fight with greed, ego, anger, jealousy, hatred —you cannot kill them, you cannot crush them, you cannot fight with them. All that you can do is just be aware of them—and the moment you are aware, they are gone. In the light, the darkness simply disappears.

Conscience

Society goes on telling you, "This is right, and that is wrong"—that is conscience. It becomes ingrained, implanted in you. You go on repeating it. That is worthless; that is not the real thing. The real thing is your own consciousness. It carries no ready-made answers about what is wrong and what is right, no. But immediately, in whatever situation arises, it gives you light —you know immediately what to do.

Conscience

Mary Magdalene and the Priceless Perfume

Jesus went to visit the home of Mary Magdalene. Mary was deeply in love. She poured very precious perfume on his feet—the whole bottle. It was rare perfume; it could have been sold. Judas immediately objected. He said, "You should prohibit people from doing such nonsense. The whole thing is wasted, and there are people who are poor and who don't have anything to eat. We could have distributed the money to poor people."

What did Jesus say? He said, "You don't be worried about it. The poor and the hungry will always be here, but I will be gone. You can serve them always and always—there is no hurry—but I will be gone. Look at the love, not at the precious perfume. Look at Mary's love, her heart."

With whom will you agree? Jesus seems to be very bourgeois and Judas seems to be perfectly economical. Judas is talking about the poor, and Jesus simply says, "I will be gone soon, so let her heart do whatsoever she wants and don't bring your philosophy in." Ordinarily your mind will agree with Judas. He was a very cultured man—sophisticated, a thinker. And he betrayed—he sold Jesus for thirty silver pieces.

But when Jesus was crucified, he started feeling guilty. That's how a good man functions—he started feeling very guilty, his conscience started pricking him. He committed suicide. He was a good man, he had a conscience. But he had no consciousness.

This distinction has to be felt deeply. Conscience is borrowed, given by the society; consciousness is your attainment. The society teaches you what is right and what is wrong: do this and don't do that. It gives you the morality, the code, the rules of the game—that is your conscience. Outside, the constable; inside, the conscience—that is how the society controls you.

Judas had a conscience, but Jesus had consciousness. Jesus was more concerned with the love of the woman, Mary Magdalene. It was such a deep thing that to prevent her would be wounding her love; she would shrink within herself. Pouring the perfume on Jesus' feet was just a gesture. Behind it, she was saying. "This is all that I have—the most precious thing I have. To pour water won't be enough; it is too cheap. I would like to pour my heart, I would like to pour my whole being...."

But Judas was a man of conscience: he looked at the perfume and he said, "It is costly." He was completely blind to the woman and her heart. The material is the perfume, the immaterial is the love. But the immaterial Judas could not see. For that, you need eyes of consciousness.

The Foolish Heart

The heart has its own reasons, which the mind cannot understand. The heart has its own dimension of being, which is completely dark for the mind. The heart is higher and deeper than the mind, beyond the reach of it. It looks foolish. Love always looks foolish because love is not utilitarian. Mind is utilitarian. It uses everything for something else—that is the meaning of being utilitarian. Mind is purposive, end-oriented; it turns everything into a means—and love cannot be turned into a means, that is the problem. Love in itself is the goal.

The Foolish Heart

The Crazy Wisdom of Francis of Assisi

Fools always have a subtle wisdom in them, and the wise always act like fools.

In the old days all great emperors always had one fool in their court. They had many wise men, counselors, ministers and prime ministers, but always one fool. Why?—because there are things so-called wise men will not be able to understand, that only a foolish man can understand—because the so-called wise are so foolish that their cunningness and cleverness closes their minds.

A fool is simple, and was needed because many times the so-called wise would not say something because they were afraid of the emperor. A fool is not afraid of anybody else, he will speak whatsoever the consequences. This is how fools act—simply, without thinking what the result will be. A clever man always thinks first of the result, then he acts. Thought comes first, then action. A foolish man acts; thought never comes first.

Whenever someone realizes the ultimate, he is not like your wise men. He cannot be. He may be like your fools, but he cannot be like your wise men.

When Saint Francis became enlightened he used to call himself "God's fool." The pope was a wise man, and when Saint Francis went to see him even the pope thought this man had gone mad. He was intelligent, calculating, clever; otherwise how could he be a pope? To become a pope one has to pass through much politics. To become a pope diplomacy is needed, a competitive aggression is needed to put others aside, to use others as ladders and then throw them. It is politics... because a pope is a political head. Religion is secondary, or nothing at all. How can a religious man fight and be aggressive for a post? They are only politicians.

Saint Francis came to see the pope, and the pope thought this man was a fool. But trees and birds and fishes thought in a different way. When Saint Francis went to the river the fishes would jump in celebration that Francis had come. Thousands witnessed this phenomenon—millions of fishes would jump simultaneously; the whole river would be lost in jumping fishes. Saint Francis had come and the fishes were happy. And wherever he would go birds would follow; they would come and sit on his leg, on his body, in his lap. They understood this fool better than the pope. Even trees that had become dry and were going to die would become green and blossom again if Saint Francis came near. These trees understood well that this fool was no ordinary fool—he was God's fool.

Prayer

Let your gestures be alive, spontaneous. Let your own awareness decide your lifestyle, life pattern. Don't allow anybody else to decide it. That is a sin, to allow anybody else to decide it. Why is it a sin?—because you will never be in it. It will remain superficial, it will be hypocrisy.

Don't ask anybody how to pray. Let the moment decide, let the moment be decisive, and the truth of the moment should be your prayer. And once you allow the truth of the moment to possess you, you will start growing and you will know tremendous beauties of prayer. You have entered on the path.

Prayer

Love and the Law of Moses

A famous story about Moses:

He was passing through a forest and he saw a man praying. The man was saying such absurd things that Moses had to stop. What the man was saying was profane, sacrilegious. He was saying, "God, you must be feeling sometimes very alone—I can come and be always with you like a shadow. Why suffer loneliness when I am here? And I am not a useless person either—I will give you a good bath, and I will take all the lice from your hair and your body..."

Lice?! Moses could not believe his ears: what is this man talking about? "And I will cook food for you—everybody likes what I cook. And I will prepare your bed and I will wash your clothes. When you are ill I will take care of you. I will be a mother to you, a wife to you, a servant, a slave—I can be all kinds of things. Just give me a hint so I can come..."

Moses stopped him and said, "What are you doing? To whom are you talking? Lice in God's hair? He needs a bath? Stop this nonsense! This is not prayer. God will be offended by you."

Looking at Moses, the man fell at his feet. He said, "I am sorry. I am an illiterate, ignorant man. I don't know how to pray. Please, you teach me!"

So Moses taught him the right way to pray, and he was very happy because he had put a man on the right track. Happy, puffed up in his ego, Moses went away.

And when he was alone in the forest, a thundering voice came from the sky and said, "Moses, I have sent you into the world to bring people to me, to bridge people with me, but not to take my lovers away from me. And that's exactly what you have done. That man is one of the most intimate to me. Go back and apologize. Take your prayer back! You have destroyed the whole beauty of his dialogue. He is sincere, he is loving. His love is true. Whatsoever he was saying, he was saying from his heart, it was not a ritual. Now what you have given to him is just a ritual. He will repeat it but it will be only on the lips; it will not be coming from his being."

Misuse of Power

The only antidote for the misuse of psychic powers is love; otherwise all power corrupts. It may be wealth, it may be prestige, it may be politics, or it may be psychic—it makes no difference. Whenever you feel powerful, if you don't have love as an antidote your power is going to become a calamity to others, a curse; because power blinds the eyes. Love opens the eyes, love cleanses the eyes... your perception becomes clear.

24

Misuse of Power

How Vivekananda Lost His Key

In Ramakrishna's ashram in Dakshineshwar, in Calcutta, there were many disciples, and Vivekananda was one of the most intellectual. There was a very simple man who was also a disciple—his name was Kalu, a poor man. He was so faithful, religious, emotional, that he had in his room hundreds of statues of different gods. Early in the morning he would take a bath in the Ganges, and then the worship of these gods would begin—and of course each had to be worshipped equally; otherwise somebody may feel offended. So Kalu's whole day was lost, and everybody was laughing at him: "What are you doing? Just one god is enough!"

Vivekananda was the most prominent in making a fool of Kalu. He said, "You are simply stupid—these are just stones! And you are wasting your life."

One day Ramakrishna gave Vivekananda a certain method of awareness to practice: "Go into your cell, close the door and practice it." When Vivekananda came to a certain stage, he felt himself so full of power that the idea came to his mind, "If I say at this moment just within myself, to Kalu, 'Take all your gods and throw them into the Ganges,' he will do it."

And he did it, he said—in his own cell, just within himself—"Kalu, just collect all your gods and throw them all into the Ganges."

Kalu collected all his gods into a big bag and was dragging the bag down the steps when Ramakrishna ran after him and said, "What are you doing?"

Kalu said, "Suddenly I heard a voice—it must have come from God himself, because there was nobody in the room—saying, 'Kalu, collect all your gods and throw them into the Ganges.' It was so powerful that I could not doubt it."

Ramakrishna said, "Come. Bring your gods back and I will show you from where the voice has come." He knocked on Vivekananda's door. Vivekananda came out and Ramakrishna was very angry. He said, "Vivekananda, this is the last thing I had ever expected of you. I had told you to be aware—not to destroy a poor man's life. He is so simple-hearted, so loving, such a beautiful man—how could you do it? From now onwards you will never attain to the same power again."

And it is said Vivekananda died without attaining enlightenment. Although he became Ramakrishna's successor because he was a great orator, had a certain charisma, influenced people, he himself died a poor man, knowing nothing. And the reason was that he disturbed a simple-hearted man because he got just a little power and he immediately used it—not for the benefit of somebody, but to harm somebody.

Light on the Path

A flash of lightning does not light your path, it does not serve you like a lamp in your hand; it only gives you a flash, a glimpse of the road ahead. But this single glimpse is very precious; now your feet are firm, now your will is strong, now your resolve to reach your destination is strengthened. You have seen the road and you know it is there and that you are not wandering aimlessly. One flash of lightning and you get a glimpse of the road you have to travel, and of the temple that is your journey's destination.

LIGHT ON THE PATH

THE PHILOSOPHER, THE MYSTIC AND THE THUNDERSTORM

I have heard about two men who were lost in a forest on a very dark night. It was a very dangerous forest, full of wild animals, very dense, with darkness all around. One man was a philosopher and the other was a mystic. Suddenly, there was a storm, a crashing of the clouds, and great lightning.

The philosopher looked at the sky, the mystic looked at the path. In that moment of lightning, the path was before him, illuminated. The philosopher looked at the lightning, and started wondering, "What is happening?" and missed the path.

You are lost in a forest denser than that of the story. The night is darker. Sometimes a flash of lightning comes—look at the path.

A Chuang Tzu is lightning, a Buddha is lightning, I am lightning. Don't look at me, look at the path. If you look at me, you have already missed, because lightning will not continue. It lasts only for a moment—and the moment is rare when eternity penetrates time; it is just like lightning.

If you look at the lightning, if you look at a buddha—and a buddha is beautiful, the face fascinates, the eyes are magnetic—if you look at the buddha, you have missed the path.

Look at the path, forget the buddha. Look at the path and do something—follow the path, act. Thinking will not lead you, only action, because thinking goes on in the head. It can never become total; only when you act, it is total.

Become interested in life!—living is the real thing. Don't go on collecting information about what meditation is—meditate! Don't go on collecting information about what dancing is—there are encyclopedias on dance, but the whole thing is utterly meaningless if you don't dance yourself.

Throw all those encyclopedias! Unburden yourself from knowledge and start living. And when you start living, then ordinary things are transformed into extraordinary beauty. Just small things—life consists of small things—but when you bring the quality of intense, passionate love they are transformed, they become luminous.

Uniqueness

Every human being is unique. There is no question of anybody superior or anybody inferior. Yes, people are different. Let me remind you of one thing; otherwise you will misunderstand me. I am not saying that everybody is equal. Nobody is superior, nobody is inferior, but nobody is equal either. People are simply unique, incomparable. You are you, I am I. I have to contribute my potential to life, you have to contribute your potential to life. I have to discover my own being, you have to discover your own being.

UNIQUENESS

BEYOND SUPERIORITY AND INFERIORITY

When inferiority disappears, all feeling of superiority also disappears. They live together, they cannot be separated. The man who feels superior is still feeling inferior somewhere. The man who feels inferior wants to feel superior somewhere. They come in a pair; they are always there together; they cannot be separated.

It happened...

A very proud man, a warrior, a samurai, came to see a Zen master. The samurai was very famous, well known all over the country, But looking at the master, looking at the beauty of the master and the grace of the moment, he suddenly felt inferior. Maybe he had come with an unconscious desire to prove his superiority.

He said to the master "Why am I feeling inferior? Just a moment ago, everything was okay. As I entered into your court suddenly I felt inferior. I have never felt like that. My hands are shaking. I am a warrior, I have faced death many times, and I have never felt any fear—why am I feeling frightened?"

The master said, "You wait. When everybody has gone, I will answer." People continued coming to visit the master, and the man was getting tired, more and more tired. By the evening the room was empty, there was nobody, and the samurai said, "Now, can you answer it?" And the master said, "Now, come outside."

A full moon night—the moon was just rising on the horizon... And he said, "Look at these trees, this tree high in the sky and this small tree. They both have existed by the side of my window for years, and there has never been any problem. The smaller tree has never said, 'Why do I feel inferior before you?' to the big tree. How is it possible? This tree is small, and that tree is big, and I have never heard any whisper."

The samurai said, "Because they can't compare."

The master said, "Then you need not ask me; you know the answer."

Comparison brings inferiority, superiority. When you don't compare, all inferiority, all superiority, disappear. Then you are, you are simply there. A small bush or a big high tree—it doesn't matter; you are yourself. You are needed. A grass leaf is needed as much as the biggest star. Without the grass leaf God will be less than he is. The sound of the cuckoo is needed as much as any Buddha; the world will be less, will be less rich if the cuckoo disappears.

Just look around. All is needed, and everything fits together. It is an organic unity: nobody is higher and nobody is lower, nobody superior, nobody inferior. Everybody is incomparably unique.

Blessings in Disguise

The only problem with sadness, desperateness, anger, hopelessness, anxiety, anguish, misery, is that you want to get rid of them. That's the only barrier. You will have to live with them. You cannot just escape. They are the very situation in which life has to integrate and grow. They are the challenges of life. Accept them. They are blessings in disguise.

Blessings in Disguise

The Fortunes and Misfortunes of a Villager

A man had a very beautiful horse, and the horse was so rare that even emperors had asked the man to sell it—whatsoever the price—but he refused. Then one morning he found that the horse had been stolen. The whole village gathered to sympathize, and they said, "How unfortunate! You could have got a fortune—people were offering so much. You were stubborn and you were stupid. Now the horse is stolen."

But the old man laughed; he said, "Don't talk nonsense! Only say that the horse is no more in the stable. Let the future come, then we will see."

And it happened that after fifteen days the horse came back, and not only alone—it brought a dozen wild horses with it from the forest. The whole village gathered, and they said, "The old man was right! His horse is back and has brought twelve beautiful horses with him. Now he can earn as much money as he wants."

They went to the man and they said, "Sorry. We could not understand the future and the ways of god, but you are great! You knew something about it; you have some glimpse of the future."

He said, "Nonsense! All that I know now is that the horse has come back with twelve horses—what is going to happen tomorrow, nobody knows."

And the next day it happened that the old man's only son was trying to break in a new horse and he fell, and his legs were broken. The whole town gathered again and they said, "One never knows—you were right; this proved to be a curse. It would have been better that the horse had not come back. Now your son will remain crippled for his whole life."

The old man said, "Don't jump ahead! Just wait and see what happens. Only say this much, that my son has broken his legs—that's all."

It happened after fifteen days that all the young men of the town were forcibly taken away by the government because the country was going to war. Only this old man's son was left, because he was of no use. Everybody gathered—they said, "Our sons are gone! At least you have your son. Maybe he is crippled, but he is here! Our sons are gone, and the enemy is far stronger; they are all going to be murdered. In our old age we will have nobody to look after us, but you at least have your son and maybe he will be cured."

But the old man said, "Say only this much—that your sons have been taken by the government. My son has been left, but there is no conclusion."

Just state the fact! Don't think of anything as a curse or a blessing. Don't interpret it, and suddenly you will see that everything is beautiful.

Self-Acceptance

You cannot improve upon yourself. And I am not saying that improvement does not happen, remember—but you cannot improve upon yourself. When you stop improving upon yourself, life improves you. In that relaxation, in that acceptance, life starts caressing you, life starts flowing through you.

Nobody else has ever been like you and nobody else will ever be like you; you are simply unique, incomparable. Accept this, love this, celebrate this—and in that very celebration you will start seeing the uniqueness of the others, the incomparable beauty of the others. Love is possible only when there is a deep acceptance of oneself, the other, the world. Acceptance creates the milieu in which love grows, the soil in which love blooms.

Self-Acceptance

Heart's-Ease in the King's Garden

I have heard:

A king went into his garden and found wilted and dying trees, shrubs and flowers. The oak said it was dying because it could not be tall like the pine. Turning to the pine, he found it drooping because it was unable to bear grapes like the vine. And the vine was dying because it could not blossom like the rose. He found Heart's-Ease blooming and as fresh as ever. Upon inquiry, he received this reply:

"I took it for granted that when you planted me you wanted Heart's-Ease. If you had desired an oak, a vine or a rose, you would have planted them. So I thought that since you put me here, I should do the best I can to be what you want. I can be nothing but what I am, and I am trying to be that to the best of my ability."

You are here because this existence needs you as you are. Otherwise somebody else would have been here!—existence would not have helped you to be here, would not have created you. You are fulfilling something very essential, something very fundamental, *as you are.*

If God wanted a Buddha he could have produced as many Buddhas as he wanted. He produced only one Buddha—that was enough, and he was satisfied to his heart's desire, utterly satisfied. Since then he has not produced another Buddha or another Christ. He has created you instead. Just think of the respect that the universe has given to you! You have been chosen, not Buddha, not Christ, not Krishna.

You will be needed more, that's why. You fit more now. Their work is done, they contributed their fragrance to existence. Now you have to contribute your fragrance.

But the moralists, the puritans, the priests, they go on teaching you, they go on driving you crazy. They say to the rose, "Become a lotus." And they say to the lotus, "What are you doing here? You have to become something else." They drive the whole garden crazy, everything starts dying—because nobody can be anybody else, that is not possible.

That's what has happened to humanity. Everybody is pretending. Authenticity is lost, truth is lost, everybody is trying to show that he is somebody else. Just look at yourself: you are pretending to be somebody else. And you can be only yourself—there is no other way, there has never been, there is no possibility that you can be anybody else. You will remain yourself. You can enjoy it and bloom, or you can wither away if you condemn it.

GRATEFULNESS

The moment one is capable of feeling grateful for both pain and pleasure, without any distinction, without any choice, simply feeling grateful for whatsoever is given... Because if it is given by God, it must have a reason in it. We may like it, we may not like it, but it must be needed for our growth. Winter and summer are both needed for growth. Once this idea settles in the heart, then each moment of life is of gratitude.

Let this become your meditation and prayer: thank God every moment—for laughter, for tears, for everything. Then you will see a silence arising in your heart that you have not known before. That is bliss.

Gratefulness

A Night Without Lodging

The first thing is to accept life as it is. Accepting it, desires disappear. Accepting life as it is, tensions disappear, discontent disappears; accepting it as it is, one starts feeling very joyful—and for no reason at all! When joy has a reason, it is not going to last long. When joy is without any reason, it is going to be there forever.

It happened in the life of a very famous Zen woman. Her name was Rengetsu.... Very few women have attained to the Zen ultimate. This one is one of those rare women.

She was on a pilgrimage and she came to a village at sunset and begged for lodging for the night, but the villagers slammed their doors. They were against Zen. Zen is so revolutionary, so utterly rebellious, that it is very difficult to accept it. By accepting it you are going to be transformed; by accepting it you will be passing through a fire, you will never be the same again. Traditional people have always been against all that is true in religion. Tradition is all that is untrue in religion. So those must have been traditional Buddhists in the town, and they didn't allow this woman to stay in the town; they threw her out.

It was a cold night, and the old woman was without lodging, and hungry. She had to make her shelter underneath a cherry tree in the fields. It was really cold, and she could not sleep well. And it was dangerous too —wild animals and all. At midnight she awoke—because of too much cold—and saw, in the night sky, the fully-opened cherry blossoms laughing to the misty moon. Overcome with the beauty, she got up and bowed down in the direction of the village, with these words:

Through their kindness
in refusing me lodging
I found myself beneath the blossoms
on the night of this misty moon.

She feels grateful. With great gratitude she thanks those people who refused her lodging; otherwise she would be sleeping under an ordinary roof and she would have missed this blessing—these cherry blossoms, and this whispering with the misty moon, and this silence of the night, this utter silence of the night. She is not angry, she accepts it. Not only accepts it, welcomes it—she feels grateful.

One becomes a buddha the moment one accepts all that life brings, with gratitude.

THAT WHICH NEVER DIES

Remember, each moment, what you are accumulating—is it going to be taken away by death? Then it is not worth bothering about. If it is not going to be taken away by death, then even life can be sacrificed for it—because one day or another life is going to disappear. Before life disappears, use the opportunity to find that which never dies.

That Which Never Dies

The Grieving Mother and the Mustard Seeds

A woman's husband died. She was young, had only one child. She wanted to commit sati, she wanted to jump in the funeral pyre with her husband, but this small child prevented her. She had to live for this small child.

But then the small child died; now it was too much. She went almost insane, asking people, "Is there any physician anywhere who can make my child alive again? I was living only for him, now my whole life is simply dark."

It happened that Buddha was coming to the town, so people said, "You take the child to Buddha. Tell him that you were living for this child, and the child has died, and ask him, 'You are such a great enlightened person, call him back to life! Have mercy on me!'"

So she went to Buddha. She put the dead body of the child at Buddha's feet and she said, "Call him back to life. You know all the secrets of life, you have attained to the ultimate peak of existence. Can't you do a small miracle for a poor woman?"

Buddha said, "I will do it, but there is a condition."

She said, "I will fulfill any condition."

Buddha said, "The condition is, you go around the town and from a house where nobody has ever died, bring a few mustard seeds."

The woman could not understand the strategy. She went to one house, and they said, "A few mustard seeds? We can bring a few bullock carts full of mustard seeds if Buddha can bring your son back to life. But we have seen so many deaths in our family...." It was a small village, and she went to every house. Everybody was ready: "How many seeds do you want?" But the condition was impossible because they had all seen so many deaths in their families....

By the evening she understood that whoever is born is going to die, so what is the point of getting the child back again? "He will die again. It is better for you yourself to seek the eternal, which is never born and never dies." She came back, empty-handed. Buddha asked, "Where are the mustard seeds?"

She laughed. In the morning she had come crying; now she laughed, and she said, "You tricked me! Everybody who is born is going to die. There is no family in the whole world where nobody has died. So I don't want my son to be brought again back to life—what is the point? Forget about the child. Initiate me into the art of meditation so that I can go into the land, the space of immortality, where birth and death have never happened."

This I call an authentic miracle: cutting the problem from the very roots.

Detachment

Go on feeling something in you that is the same no matter what happens on the periphery. When someone is insulting you, focus yourself to the point where you are just listening to him—not doing anything, not reacting, just listening. He is insulting you. And then someone is praising you—just listen. Insult-praise, honor-dishonor, just listen. Your periphery will get disturbed. Look at that also, don't try to change it. Look at it; remain deep in your center, looking from there. You will have a detachment which is not forced, which is spontaneous, which is natural. And once you have the feeling of the natural detachment, nothing can disturb you.

Detachment

Hakuin and the Infant Child

In a village where the great Zen master Hakuin was living, a girl became pregnant. Her father bullied her for the name of her lover and, in the end, to escape punishment she told him it was Hakuin.

The father said no more, but when the time came and the child was born, he at once took the baby to Hakuin and threw it down. "It seems that this is your child," he said, and he piled on every insult and sneer at the disgrace of the affair.

Hakuin only said, "Oh, is that so?" and took the baby in his arms. Wherever he went thereafter, he took the baby, wrapped in the sleeve of his ragged robe. During rainy days and stormy nights he would go out to beg milk from the neighboring houses. Many of his disciples, considering him fallen, turned against him and left. And Hakuin said not a word.

Meantime, the mother found she could not bear the agony of separation from her child. She confessed the name of the real father, and her own father rushed to Hakuin and prostrated himself, begging over and over for forgiveness.

Hakuin said only, "Oh, is that so?" and gave him the child back.

For the ordinary man what others say matters too much, because he has nothing of his own. Whatever he thinks he is, is just a collection of opinions of other people. Somebody has said, "You are beautiful," somebody has said, "You are intelligent," and he has been collecting all these. Hence he's always afraid: he should not behave in such a way that he loses his reputation, respectability. He is always afraid of public opinion, what people will say, because all that he knows about himself is what people have said about him. If they take it back, they leave him naked. Then he does not know who he is, ugly, beautiful, intelligent, unintelligent. He has no idea, even vaguely, of his own being; he depends on others.

But the man of meditation has no need of others' opinions. He knows himself, so it does not matter what others say. Even if the whole world says something that goes against his own experience, he will simply laugh. At the most, that can be the only response. But he is not going to take any step to change people's opinion. Who are they? They don't know themselves and they are trying to label him. He will reject labeling. He will simply say, "Whatever I am, I am, and this is the way I am going to be."

Beyond the Small Family

You are born with a tremendous possibility of intelligence. You are born with a light within you. Listen to the still, small voice within, and that will guide you. Nobody else can guide you, nobody else can become a model for your life, because you are unique. Nobody has there ever been who was exactly like you, and nobody is ever going to be there again who will be exactly like you. This is your glory, your grandeur—that you are utterly irreplaceable, that you are just yourself and nobody else.

Beyond the Small Family

"No one is my mother..."

Jesus was a small child and his father and mother had come to the great temple for the annual festival. Jesus was lost somewhere in the crowd, and only by the evening could his parents find him. He was sitting with some scholars, just a child, and he was discussing things with them. His father said, "Jesus, what are you doing here? We have been worried about you."

Jesus said, "Don't be worried. I was looking after my father's business."

The father said, "I am your father—and what type of business are you looking after here? I am a carpenter."

Jesus said, "My father is in heaven. You are not my father."

Just as a child has to leave the body of the mother, otherwise he will be dead—he has to come out of the womb—the same happens mentally, also. One day he has to come out of the father and mother's womb. Not only physically but mentally; not only mentally but spiritually. And when the spiritual child is born, has broken with his past completely, for the first time he becomes a self, an independent reality, standing on his own feet. Before this he was just a part of the mother, or the father, or the family—but he was never himself.

Whatever you are doing, whatever you are thinking, whatever you are deciding, look: is it coming from you or is somebody else speaking? And you will be surprised to find out the real voice; perhaps it is your mother—you will hear her speak again. Perhaps it is your father; it is not at all difficult to detect. It remains there, recorded in you exactly as it was given to you for the first time—the advice, the order, the discipline, the commandment.

You may find many people, the priest, the teachers, the friends, the neighbors, the relatives. There is no need to fight. Just knowing that it is not your voice but somebody else's—whosoever that somebody else is—you know that you are not going to follow it. Whatsoever the consequences, now you are deciding to move on your own, you are deciding to be mature. Enough you have remained a child. Enough you have remained dependent. Enough you have listened to all these voices and followed them. And where have they brought you? In a mess.

So once you figure out whose voice it is, say goodbye to it... because the person who gave that voice to you was not your enemy. His intention was not bad, but it is not a question of his intention. The question is that he imposed something on you that is not coming from your own inner source; and anything that comes from outside makes you a psychological slave. It is only your own voice that will lead you into a blossoming, into freedom.

Renewal

When there is no past, when there is no future, only then is there peace. Future means aspirations, achievement, goal, ambition, desire. You cannot be here now, you are always rushing for something, somewhere else. One has to be utterly present to the present, then there is peace. And out of that is renewal of life, because life knows only one time, and that is the present. The past is death; the future is just a projection of the dead past. What can you think about the future? You think in terms of the past, that's what you know, and you project it—of course in a better way. It is more beautiful, decorated; all the pains have been dropped and only the pleasures have been chosen, but it is the past. The past is not, the future is not, only the present is. To be in the present is to be alive, optimum—and that is renewal.

Renewal

The Heritage of the Buddha

Just one day before Gautam Buddha left his palace to seek the truth, a child had been born to his wife. It is such a human story, so beautiful… Before leaving the palace he just wanted to see at least once the face of his child, the symbol of his love with his wife. So he went into the chamber of his wife. She was asleep, and the child was covered, under a blanket. He wanted to remove the blanket and to see the face of the child, because perhaps he would never come back again.

He was going on an unknown pilgrimage. He was risking everything, his kingdom, his wife, his child, himself, in search of enlightenment—something he has only heard of as a possibility, which has happened before to a few people who have looked for it. He was as full of doubts as any one of you, but the moment of decision had come. He was determined to leave. But the human mind, human nature... He just wanted to see—he had not even seen the face of his own child. But he was afraid that if he removes the blanket, if Yashodhara, his wife, wakes up she will ask, "What are you doing in the middle of the night in my room?—and you seem to be ready to go somewhere."

He was just about to leave, and he had said to his charioteer, "Just wait a minute. Let me see the child's face. I may never come back again." But he could not look because of the fear that if Yashodhara wakes up, starts crying, weeping, "Where are you going? What are you doing? What is this renunciation? What is this enlightenment?" One never knows about a woman—she may wake up the whole palace! His father will come, and the whole thing will be spoiled. So he simply escaped...

After twelve years, when he was enlightened, the first thing he did was to come back to his palace to apologize to his father, to his wife, to his son who must be now twelve years of age. He was aware that they would be angry. The father was very angry—he was the first one to meet him, and for half an hour he continued abusing Buddha. But then suddenly he became aware that he was saying so many things and his son was just standing there like a marble statue, as if nothing was affecting him. The father looked at him, and Gautam Buddha said, "That's what I wanted. Please dry your tears. Look at me: I am not the same boy who left the palace. Your son died long ago. I look similar to your son, but my whole consciousness is different. You just look."

The father said, "I am seeing it. For half an hour I have been abusing you, and that is enough proof that you have changed. Otherwise I know how temperamental you were: you could not stand so silently. What has happened to you?"

Renewal

Buddha said, "I will tell you. Just let me first see my wife and my child. They must be waiting—they must have heard that I have come."

And the first thing his wife said to him was, "I can see that you are transformed. These twelve years were a great suffering, but not because you had gone; I suffered because you did not tell me. If you had simply told me that you were going to seek the truth, do you think I would have prevented you? You have insulted me very badly. This is the wound that I have been carrying for twelve years. I also belong to the warrior caste—do you think I am that weak that I would have cried and screamed and stopped you?

"All these twelve years my only suffering was that you did not trust me. I would have allowed you, I would have given you a send off, I would have come up to the chariot. First I want to ask the only question that has been in my mind for all these twelve years, which is that whatever you have attained... and it certainly seems you have attained something.

"You are no longer the same person who left this palace; you radiate a different light, your presence is totally new and fresh, your eyes are as pure and clear as a cloudless sky. You have become so beautiful... you were always beautiful, but this beauty seems to be not of this world. Some grace from the beyond has descended on you. My question is that whatever you have attained, was it not possible to attain it here in this palace? Can the palace prevent the truth?"

It is a tremendously intelligent question, and Gautam Buddha had to agree: "I could have attained it here but I had no idea at that moment. Now I can say that I could have attained it here in this palace; there was no need to go to the mountains, there was no need to go anywhere. I had to go inside, and that could have happened anywhere. This palace was as good as any other place, but now I can say that at that moment I had no idea.

"So you have to forgive me, because it is not that I did not trust you or your courage. In fact, I was doubtful of myself: if I had seen you wake up and if I had seen the child, I may have started wondering, 'What am I doing, leaving my beautiful wife, whose total love, whose total devotion is for me. And leaving my one-day-old child... if I am to leave him then why did I give birth to him? I am escaping from my responsibilities.'

"If my old father had awakened, it would have become impossible for me. It was not that I did not trust you; it was really that I did not trust myself. I knew that there was a wavering; I was not total in renouncing. A part of me was saying, 'What are you doing?'—and a part of me was saying, 'This is the time to do it. If you don't do it now it will become more and more difficult. Your father is preparing to crown you. Once you are crowned as king, it will be more difficult.'"

Yashodhara said to him, "This is the only question that I wanted to ask, and I am immensely happy that you have been absolutely truthful in saying that it can be attained here, it can be attained anywhere. Now your son, who is just standing there, a little boy of twelve years, has been continually asking about you, and I have been telling him, 'Just wait. He will come back; he cannot be so cruel, he cannot be so unkind, he cannot be so inhuman. One day he will come. Perhaps whatever he has gone to realize is taking time; once he has realized it, the first thing he will do is to come back.'

"So your son is here, and I want you to tell me what heritage you are leaving for your son? What have you got to give him? You have given him life—now what else?"

Buddha had nothing except his begging bowl, so he called his son, whose name was Rahul. He called Rahul close to him and gave him the begging bowl. He said, "I don't have anything. This is my only possession; from now onwards I will have to use my hands as a begging bowl to take my food, to beg my food. By giving you this begging bowl I am initiating you into sannyas. That is the only treasure that I have found, and I would like you to find it too."

He said to Yashodhara, "You have to be ready to become a part of my commune of sannyasins," and he initiated his wife. The old man had come and was watching the whole scene. He said to Gautam Buddha, "Then why are you leaving me out? Don't you want to share what you have found with your old father? My death is very close... initiate me also."

Buddha said, "I had come, in fact, just to take you all with me, because what I have found is a far greater kingdom—a kingdom that is going to last forever, which cannot be conquered. I had come here so that you could feel my presence, so that you could feel my realization, and I could persuade you to become my fellow-travelers."

Anger

Next time you feel angry, go and run around the house seven times, and afterwards sit under a tree and watch where the anger has gone. You have not repressed it, you have not controlled it, you have not thrown it on somebody else....

Anger is just a mental vomit. There is just no need to throw it on somebody. Do a little jogging, or take a pillow and beat the pillow until your hands and teeth are relaxed.

In transformation you never control, you simply become more aware. Anger is happening—it is a beautiful phenomenon, it is just like electricity in the clouds....

ANGER

THE MONK WITH THE UNGOVERNABLE TEMPER

A Zen student came to Bankei and said, "Master, I have an ungovernable temper. How can I cure it?" "Show me this temper," said Bankei, "it sounds fascinating." "I haven't got it right now," said the student, "so I can't show it to you."

"Well then," said Bankei, "bring it to me when you have it."

"But I can't bring it just when I happen to have it," protested the student. "It arises unexpectedly, and I would surely lose it before I got it to you."

"In that case," said Bankei, "it cannot be part of your true nature. If it were, you could show it to me at any time. When you were born you did not have it—so it must have come to you from the outside. I suggest that whenever it gets into you, you beat yourself with a stick until the temper can't stand it and runs away."

Even while anger is happening, if you suddenly become conscious, it drops. Try it! Just in the middle, when you are very hot and would like to murder—suddenly become aware, and you will feel something has changed: a gear inside, you can feel the click, your inner being has relaxed. It may take time for your outer layer to relax, but the inner being has already relaxed. The cooperation has broken...now you are not identified.

The body will take a little time to cool down, but deep at the center everything is cool.

Awareness is needed, not condemnation—and through awareness transformation happens spontaneously. If you become aware of your anger, understanding penetrates. Just watching, with no judgment, not saying good, not saying bad, just watching in your inner sky. There is lightning, anger, you feel hot, the whole nervous system shaking and quaking, and you feel a tremor all over the body—a beautiful moment, because when energy functions you can watch it easily; when it is not functioning you cannot watch.

Close your eyes and meditate on it. Don't fight, just look at what is happening—the whole sky filled with electricity, so much lightning, so much beauty—just lie down on the ground and look at the sky and watch. Then do the same inside.

Somebody has insulted you, somebody has laughed at you, somebody has said this or that... many clouds, dark clouds in the inner sky and much lightning. Watch! It is a beautiful scene—terrible also, because you don't understand. It is mysterious, and if mystery is not understood it becomes terrible, you are afraid of it. And whenever a mystery is understood, it becomes a grace, a gift, because now you have the keys—and with keys you are the master.

Mastery of Moods

To think that "I am the mind," is unawareness. To know that mind is only a mechanism just as the body is, to know that the mind is separate.... The night comes, the morning comes: you don't get identified with the night. You don't say, "I am night," you don't say, "I am morning." The night comes, the morning comes, the day comes, again the night comes; the wheel goes on moving, but you remain alert that you are not these things. The same is the case with the mind. Anger comes, but you forget—you become anger. Greed comes, you forget—you become greed. Hate comes, you forget—you become hate. This is unawareness.

Awareness is watching that the mind is full of greed, full of anger, full of hate or full of lust, but you are simply a watcher. Then you can see greed arising, becoming a great, dark cloud, then dispersing—and you remain untouched. How long can it remain? Your anger is momentary, your greed is momentary, your lust is momentary. Just watch a little and you will be surprised: it comes and it goes. And you are remaining there unaffected, cool, calm.

Mastery of Moods

The Secret of the Ring

The most basic thing to remember is that when you are feeling good, in a mood of ecstasy, don't start thinking that it is going to be your permanent state. Live the moment as joyfully, as cheerfully as possible, knowing perfectly well that it has come and it will go—just like a breeze comes in your house, with all its fragrance and freshness, and goes out from the other door.

This is the most fundamental thing. If you start thinking in terms of making your ecstatic moments permanent, you have already started destroying them. When they come, be grateful; when they leave, be thankful to existence. Remain open. It will happen many times—don't be judgmental, don't be a chooser. Remain choiceless.

Yes, there will be moments when you will be miserable. So what? There are people who are miserable and who have not even known a single moment of ecstasy; you are fortunate. Even in your misery, remember that it is not going to be permanent; it will also pass away, so don't get too much disturbed by it. Remain at ease. Just like day and night, there are moments of joy and there are moments of sadness; accept them as part of the duality of nature, as the very way things are.

And you are simply a watcher: neither you become happiness nor you become misery. Happiness comes and goes, misery comes and goes. One thing remains always there—always and always—and that is the watcher, one who witnesses. Slowly, slowly get more and more centered into the watcher. Days will come and nights will come... lives will come and deaths will come... success will come, failure will come. But if you are centered in the watcher —because that is the only reality in you—everything is a passing phenomenon.

Just for a moment, try to feel what I am saying: just be a watcher.... Do not cling to any moment because it is beautiful, and do not push any moment because it is miserable. Stop doing that. That you have been doing for lives. You have not been successful yet and you will never be successful ever.

The only way to go beyond, to remain beyond, is to find a place from where you can watch all these changing phenomena without getting identified.

I will tell you an ancient Sufi story...

A king asked his wise men in the court, "I am making a very beautiful ring for myself. I have got one of the best diamonds possible. I want to keep hidden inside the ring some message that may be helpful to me in a time of utter despair. It has to be very small so that it can be hidden underneath the diamond in the ring."

They were all wise men, they all were great scholars;

Mastery of Moods

they could have written great treatises. But to give him a message of not more than two or three words which would help him in moments of utter despair... They thought, they looked into their books, but they could not find anything.

The king had an old servant who was almost like his father—he had been his father's servant. The king's mother had died early and this servant had taken care of him, so he was not treated like a servant. The king had immense respect for him.

The old man said, "I am not a wise man, knowledgeable, scholarly; but I know the message—because there is only one message. And these people cannot give it to you; it can be given only by a mystic, by a man who has realized himself.

"In my long life in the palace I have come across all kinds of people, and once, a mystic. He had also been a guest of your father and I was put into his service. When he was departing, as a gesture of thankfulness for all my services he gave me this message"—and he wrote it on a small piece of paper, folded it and told the king, "Don't read it, just keep it hidden in the ring. Only open it when everything else has failed—when there is no way out."

And the time came soon. The country was invaded and the king lost his kingdom. He was running away on his horse just to save his life and the enemy horses were following him. He was alone; they were many. And he came to a place where the path stopped, came to a dead end; there was a cliff and a deep valley. To fall into it was to be finished. He could not go back, the enemy was there and he could hear the sounds of the hooves of the horses. He could not go forward, and there was no other way....

Suddenly he remembered the ring. He opened it, took out the paper, and there was a small message of tremendous value: it simply said, "This too will pass." A great silence came over him as he read the sentence, "This too will pass." And it passed.

Everything passes away; nothing remains in this world. The enemies who were following him must have got lost in the forest, must have moved on a wrong way; the hooves slowly, slowly were not heard any more.

The king was immensely grateful to the servant and to the unknown mystic. Those words proved miraculous. He folded the paper, put it back into the ring, gathered his armies again and conquered his kingdom back. And the day he was entering his capital, victorious, there was great celebration all over the capital, music, dance—and he was feeling very proud of himself.

The old man was walking by the side of his chariot.

Mastery of Moods

He said, "This time is also right: look again at the message."

The king said, "What do you mean? Now I am victorious, people are celebrating. I am not in despair, I am not in a situation where there is no way out."

The old man said, "Listen. This is what the saint has said to me: this message is not only for despair, it is also for pleasure. This is not only for when you are defeated; it is also for when you are victorious—not only when you are the last, but also when you are the first."

And the king opened the ring, read the message, "This too will pass," and suddenly the same peace, the same silence, amidst the crowds, jubilating, celebrating, dancing... but the pride, the ego was gone.

Everything passes away.

He asked his old servant to come on the chariot and sit with him. He asked, "Is there anything more? Everything passes away... Your message has been immensely helpful."

The old man said, "The third thing the saint said, 'Remember, everything passes. Only you remain; you remain forever as a witness.'"

Everything passes, but you remain. You are the reality; everything else is just a dream. Beautiful dreams are there, nightmares are there... But it does not matter whether it is a beautiful dream or a nightmare; what matters is the one who is seeing the dream. That seer is the only reality.

The Gates of Hell

Heaven and hell are not geographical, they are psychological, they are your psychology. Heaven and hell are not at the end of your life, they are here and now. Every moment the door opens; every moment you go on wavering between heaven and hell. It is a moment-to-moment question, it is urgent; in a single moment you can move from hell to heaven, from heaven to hell.

Hell and heaven are within you. The doors are very close to each other: with the right hand you can open one, with the left hand you can open another. With just a change of your mind, your being is transformed —from heaven to hell and from hell to heaven. Whenever you act unconsciously, without awareness, you are in hell; whenever you are conscious, whenever you act with full awareness, you are in heaven.

The Gates of Hell/Gates of Heaven

The Samurai's Pride

The Zen master Hakuin is one of the rare flowerings. A warrior came to him, a samurai, a great soldier, and he asked "Is there any hell, is there any heaven? If there is hell and heaven, where are the gates? Where do I enter from? How can I avoid hell and choose heaven?" He was a simple warrior. A warrior is always simple; otherwise he cannot be a warrior. A warrior knows only two things, life and death—his life is always at stake, he is always gambling; He is a simple man. He had not come to learn any doctrine. He wanted to know where the gate was so he could avoid hell and enter heaven.

And Hakuin replied in a way only a warrior could understand. What did Hakuin do? He said, "Who are you?" And the warrior replied, "I am a samurai." It is a thing of much pride to be a samurai in Japan. It means being a perfect warrior, a man who will not hesitate a single moment to give his life. For him, life and death are just a game.

He said, "I am a samurai, I am a leader of samurais. Even the emperor pays respect to me."

Hakuin laughed and said, " You, a samurai? You look like a beggar."

The samurai's pride was hurt, his ego hammered. He forgot what he had come for. He took out his sword and was just about to kill Hakuin. He forgot that he had come to this master to ask where is the gate of heaven, to ask where is the gate of hell. Hakuin laughed and said, "This is the gate of hell. With this sword, this anger, this ego, here opens the gate." This is what a warrior can understand. Immediately he understood: This is the gate. He put his sword back in its sheath.

And Hakuin said, "Here opens the gate of heaven."

Hell and heaven are within you, both gates are within you. When you are behaving unconsciously there is the gate of hell; when you become alert and conscious, there is the gate of heaven.What happened to this samurai? When he was just about to kill Hakuin, was he conscious? Was he conscious of what he was about to do? Was he conscious of what he had come for? All consciousness had disappeared. When the ego takes over, you cannot be alert. Ego is the drug, the intoxicant that makes you completely unconscious. You act but the act comes from the unconscious, not from your consciousness. And whenever any act comes from the unconscious, the door of hell is open. Whatsoever you do, if you are not aware of what you are doing the gate of hell opens. Immediately the samurai became alert.

The Gates of Heaven

The Gates of Hell/Gates of Heaven

Suddenly, when Hakuin said, "This is the gate, you have already opened it"— the very situation must have created alertness.

A single moment more and Hakuin's head would have been severed; a single moment more and it would have been separated from the body. And Hakuin said, "This is the gate of hell." This is not a philosophical answer; no master answers in a philosophical way. Philosophy exists only for mediocre, unenlightened minds. The master responds but the response is not verbal, it is total. That this man may have killed him is not the point. "If you kill me and it makes you alert, it is worth it"—Hakuin played the game.

This must have happened to the warrior—stopped, sword in hand with Hakuin just before him—the eyes of Hakuin were laughing, the face was smiling, and the gate of heaven opened. He understood: the sword went back into its sheath. While putting the sword back into the sheath he must have been totally silent, peaceful. The anger had disappeared, the energy moving in anger had become silence.

If you suddenly awake in the middle of anger, you will feel a peace you have never felt before. Energy was moving and suddenly it stops—you will have silence, immediate silence. You will fall into your inner being and the fall will be so sudden, you will become aware. It is not a slow fall, it is so sudden that you cannot remain unaware. You can remain unaware only with routine things, with gradual things; you move so slowly you can't feel movement. This was sudden movement—from activity to no-activity, from thought to no-thought, from mind to no-mind.

As the sword was going back into its sheath, the warrior realized. And Hakuin said, "Here open the doors of heaven." Silence is the door. Inner peace is the door. Non-violence is the door. Love and compassion are the doors.

Transmutation

Pain is natural; it has to be understood, it has to be accepted. Because naturally we are afraid of pain, naturally we avoid it. Hence many people have avoided the heart and are hung up in the head, they live in the head. The heart gives pain, true, but only because it can give pleasure —that's why it gives pain. Pain is the way that pleasure arrives; agony, the door that ecstasy enters.

If one is aware of it, one accepts the pain as a blessing. Then suddenly the quality of the pain immediately starts changing. You are no longer antagonistic to it, and because you are no longer antagonistic to it, it is no longer pain; it is a friend. It is a fire that is going to cleanse you. It is a transmutation, a process, in which the old will go and the new will arrive, in which the mind will disappear and the heart will function in its totality. Then life is a benediction.

TRANSMUTATION

ATISHA'S HEART MEDITATION

Try this method from Atisha:

When you breathe in—listen carefully, it is one of the greatest methods—when you breathe in, think that you are breathing in all the miseries of all the people in the world. All the darkness, all the negativity, all the hell that exists anywhere, you are breathing it in. And let it be absorbed in your heart.

You may have read or heard about the so-called positive thinkers of the West. They say just the opposite —they don't know what they are saying. They say, "When you breathe out, throw out all your misery and negativity; and when you breathe in, breathe in joy, positivity, happiness, cheerfulness."

Atisha's method is just the opposite: when you breathe in, breathe in all the misery and suffering of all the beings of the world—past, present and future. And when you breathe out, breathe out all the joy that you have, all the blissfulness that you have, all the benediction that you have. Breathe out, pour yourself into existence. This is the method of compassion: drink in all the suffering and pour out all the blessings.

And you will be surprised if you do it. The moment you take all the sufferings of the world inside you, they are no longer sufferings. The heart immediately transforms the energy. The heart is a transforming force: drink in misery, and it is transformed into blissfulness... then pour it out.

Once you have learned that your heart can do this magic, this miracle, you would like to do it again and again. Try it. It is one of the most practical methods—simple, and it brings immediate results. Do it today, and see.

That is one of the approaches of Buddha and all his disciples. Atisha is one of his disciples, in the same tradition, in the same line. Buddha says again and again to his disciples, "*Ihi passiko*—come and see!" They are very scientific people. Buddhism is the most scientific religion on the earth; hence, Buddhism is gaining more and more ground in the world every day. As the world becomes more intelligent, Buddha will become more and more important. It is bound to be so. As more and more people come to know about science, Buddha will have great appeal. He will convince the scientific mind—because he says, "Whatsoever I am saying can be practiced." I don't say to you, "Believe it," I say, "Experiment with it, experience it, and only then if you feel it yourself, trust it. Otherwise there is no need to believe."

Try this beautiful method of compassion: take in all the misery and pour out all the joy.

Energy

Either you make your energy creative, or it will turn sour and become destructive. Energy is a dangerous thing—if you have it, you have to use it creatively, otherwise sooner or later you will find it has become destructive. So find something—whatsoever you like—to put your energy into. If you want, painting; or if you want, dancing or singing; or if you want to play an instrument.... Whatsoever you want, find a way in which you can become completely lost.

If you can be lost playing a guitar—good! In those moments when you are lost, your energy will be released in a creative way. If you cannot be lost in painting, in singing, in dancing, in playing guitar or a flute, then you will find lower ways of being lost: anger, rage, aggression; these are lower ways to be lost.

ENERGY

THE MAN WITH A GARLAND OF FINGERS

Gautam Buddha initiated a murderer into sannyas —and the murderer was no ordinary murderer. Rudolf Hess is nothing compared to him. His name was Angulimal. Angulimal means a man who wears a garland of human fingers.

He had taken a vow that he would kill one thousand people; from each single person he would take one finger so that he could remember how many he had killed and he will make a garland of all those fingers. In his garland of fingers he had nine hundred and ninety-nine fingers—only one was missing. And that one was missing because his road was closed; nobody was coming that way. But Gautam Buddha entered that closed road. The king had put guards on the road to prevent people, particularly strangers who didn't know that a dangerous man lived behind the hills. The guards told Gautam Buddha, "That is not the road to be used. This is the place where Angulimal lives. Even the king has not the guts to go on this road. That man is simply mad.

"His mother used to go to him. She was the only person who used to go, once in a while, to see him, but even she stopped. The last time she went there he told her, 'Now only one finger is missing, and just because you happen to be my mother... I want to warn you that if you come another time you will not go back. I need one finger desperately. Up to now I have not killed you because other people were available, but now nobody passes on this road except you. So I want to make you aware that next time if you come it will be your responsibility, not mine.' Since that time his mother has not come." The guards said to Buddha, "Don't unnecessarily take the risk."

And do you know what Buddha said to them? Buddha said, "If I don't go then who will go? Only two things are possible: either I will change him, and I cannot miss this challenge; or I will provide him with one finger so that his desire is fulfilled. Anyway I am going to die one day. Giving my head to Angulimal will be at least of some use; otherwise one day I will die and you will put me on the funeral pyre. I think that it is better to fulfill somebody's desire and give him peace of mind. Either he will kill me or I will kill him, but this encounter is going to happen; you just lead the way."

The people who used to follow Gautam Buddha, his close companions who were always in competition to be closer to him, started slowing down. Soon there were miles between Gautam Buddha and his disciples. They all wanted to see what happened, but they didn't want to be too close.

Energy

Angulimal was sitting on his rock watching. He could not believe his eyes. A very beautiful man of such immense charisma was coming towards him. Who could this man be? He had never heard of Gautam Buddha, but even this hard heart of Angulimal started feeling a certain softness towards the man. He was looking so beautiful, coming towards him. It was early morning... a cool breeze, and the sun was rising... and the birds were singing and the flowers had opened; and Buddha was coming closer and closer.

Finally Angulimal, with his naked sword in his hand, shouted, "Stop!" Gautam Buddha was just a few feet away, and Angulimal said, "Don't take another step because then the responsibility will not be mine. Perhaps you don't know who I am!"

Buddha said, "Do you know who you are?"

Angulimal said, "This is not the point. Neither is it the place nor the time to discuss such things. Your life is in danger!"

Buddha said, "I think otherwise—your life is in danger."

That man said, "I used to think I was mad—you are really mad. And you go on moving closer. Then don't say that I killed an innocent man. You look so innocent and so beautiful that I want you to go back. I will find somebody else. I can wait; there is no hurry. If I can manage nine hundred and ninety-nine... it is only a question of one more, but don't force me to kill you."

Buddha came very close, and Angulimal's hands were trembling. The man was so beautiful, so innocent, so childlike. He had already fallen in love. He had killed so many people... He had never felt this weakness; he had never known what love is. For the first time he was full of love. So there was a contradiction: the hand was holding the sword to kill the person, and his heart was saying, "Put the sword back in the sheath."

Buddha said, "I am ready, but why is your hand shaking?—you are such a great warrior, even kings are afraid of you, and I am just a poor beggar. Except the begging bowl, I don't have anything. You can kill me, and I will feel immensely satisfied that at least my death fulfills somebody's desire; my life has been useful, my death has also been useful. But before you cut my head I have a small desire, and I think you will grant me a small desire before killing me."

Before death, even the hardest enemy is willing to fulfill any desire. Angulimal said, "What do you want?"

Buddha said, "I want you just to cut from the tree a branch which is full of flowers. I will never see these flowers again; I want to see those flowers closely, feel their fragrance and their beauty in this morning sun, their glory."

So Angulimal cut with his sword a whole branch full of flowers. And before he could give it to Buddha, Buddha said, "This was only half the desire; the other half is, please put the branch back on the tree."

Angulimal said, "I was thinking from the very beginning that you are crazy. Now this is the craziest desire. How can I put this branch back?"

Buddha said, "If you cannot create, you have no right to destroy. If you cannot give life, you don't have the right to give death to any living thing."

A moment of silence and a moment of transformation... the sword fell down from his hands. Angulimal fell down at the feet of Gautam Buddha, and he said, "I don't know who you are, but whoever you are, take me to the same space in which you are; initiate me."

By that time the followers of Gautam Buddha had come closer and closer. They were all around and when he fell at Buddha's feet they immediately came close. Somebody raised the question, "Don't initiate this man, he is a murderer!"

Buddha said again, "If I don't initiate him, who will initiate him? And I love the man, I love his courage. And I can see tremendous possibility in him: a single man fighting against the whole world. I want this kind of people, who can stand against the whole world. Up to now he was standing against the world with a sword; now he will stand against the world with a consciousness, which is far sharper than any sword. I told you that murder was going to happen, but it was not certain who was going to be murdered—either I was going to be murdered, or Angulimal. Now you can see Angulimal is murdered. And who I am to judge?"

WHOLENESS

No man is an island, we are all part of a vast continent. There is variety, but that does not make us separate. Variety makes life richer—part of us is in the Himalayas, a part of us is in the stars, a part of us is in the roses. A part of us is in the bird on the wing, a part of us is in the green of the trees. We are spread all over. To experience it as reality will transform your whole approach towards life, will transform your every act, will transform your very being.

Wholeness

"Just an ordinary needle will do..."

It is reported in the life of a great Sufi mystic, Farid, that a king came to see him. He had brought a present for him, a beautiful pair of scissors, golden, studded with diamonds—very valuable, very rare. He touched Farid's feet and gave him the scissors; Farid took them, looked at them, gave them back to the king, and said, "Sir, many thanks for the present that you have brought. It is beautiful, but utterly useless for me. It will be better if you can give me a needle. Scissors I don't need; a needle will do."

The king said, "I don't understand. If you need a needle, you will need scissors too."

Farid said, "I am talking in metaphors. Scissors I don't need because scissors cut things apart. A needle I need because a needle puts things together. I teach love. My whole teaching is based on love—putting things together, teaching people communion. I need a needle so that I can put people together. The scissors are useless; they cut, they disconnect. Next time when you come, just an ordinary needle will be enough."

Logic is like a pair of scissors: it cuts, it makes things divided. Mind is a kind of prism—pass a ray of white light through it and immediately it is divided into seven colors. Pass anything through the mind and it becomes dual. Life and death are not life-and-death, the reality is lifedeath. It should be one word, not two; not even a hyphen in between. Lifedeath is one phenomenon. Lovehate is one phenomenon. Darknesslight is one phenomenon. Negativepositive is one phenomenon. But when you pass this one phenomenon through the mind, the one is divided immediately in two. Lifedeath becomes life and death—not only divided but death becomes antagonistic to life. They are enemies. Now you can go on trying to make these two meet, and they will never meet.

Kipling is right—"East is East and West is West and never the twain shall meet." Logically, it is true. How can the East meet the West? How can the West meet the East? But existentially it is utter nonsense. They are meeting everywhere. For example, you are sitting in India. Is it East or is it West? If you are comparing it with London, it is East; but if you are comparing it with Tokyo, it is West. What exactly is it, East or West? At each point East and West are meeting, and Kipling says, "Never the twain shall meet." The twain is meeting everywhere. No single point is such that East and West are not meeting and no single man is such that East and West are not meeting. It cannot be otherwise; they have to meet—it is one reality, one sky.

Failure

When it is morning, it is morning. When it is evening, it is evening. There is no question of choice. Drop the choice and you are free everywhere—freedom can be only in choicelessness. So when you are young, it is beautiful; when you are a child, it is beautiful; when you are old, it is beautiful; when you are dying, it is beautiful—because you are never separate from the total, you are just a wave in the ocean.

The wave in the ocean can start thinking of itself as an individual—then there will be trouble. The wave in the ocean never thinks of itself as separate, so wherever the ocean is taking her, she is willingly, joyously, dancingly moving in that direction.

FAILURE

THE OPEN SECRET OF REAL SUCCESS

A song from the mystic Kabir:

I talk to my inner lover and I say, why such rush? We sense that there is some sort of spirit that loves birds and animals and the ants—perhaps the same one who gave a radiance to you in your mother's womb. Is it logical you would be walking around entirely orphaned now? The truth is, you turned away yourself, and decided to go into the dark alone. Now you are tangled up in others and have forgotten what you once knew, and that is why everything you do has some weird failure in it.

Things happen when they are needed to happen; things are bound to happen when they are needed to happen. All goes well—just trust. Remember the difference. The theologian will say, "Believe in the concept of God." The mystic says there is no need to believe in the concept of God, just sense the harmony in existence. It is not a concept, it is not a belief—you can sense it, it is everywhere. It is almost tangible.

The moment you think you are one with the whole, there is relaxation; a sudden let-go happens. You need not keep hold of yourself, you can relax. There is no need to remain tense, because there is no private goal to be attained by you. You flow with God. God's goal is your goal, his destiny is your destiny. You don't have a private destiny—the private destiny brings problems.

Have you not watched it in your own life? All that you do goes on failing. You still don't see the point—you think that you didn't do it as it should have been done, that's why it has failed. So you try another project and you fail again. Then you think that your skill is not enough, so you learn the skill and then you fail again. Then you think "The whole world is against me" or "Fate is against me" or "I am a victim of people's jealousies." You go on finding explanations for why you fail, but you never strike the real ground of your failure.

Kabir says: Failure means you-minus-God. That's Kabir's understanding. Failure is equal to you-minus-God, and success is equal to you-plus-God. Success is within God and with God. And remember, by 'God' I don't mean a person sitting somewhere in heaven, but the cosmic spirit. Sense the cosmic spirit, the Tao, the law that permeates the whole existence—out of which you are born, and to which one day you will return.

Worry

Have you ever taken note of one thing?—the present is always juicy, the present is always blissful. Worry and suffering are created either by what you wanted to do in the past and could not do, or by what you want to do in the future and don't know whether you will be able to do or not. Did you ever notice, did you ever look at this small truth, that there is no suffering in the present, there is no worry? This is why the present does not disturb the mind—anxiety disturbs the mind. There is no suffering in the present. The present doesn't know suffering—the present is such a small moment that suffering cannot fit into it. In the present only heaven can fit, not hell. Hell is too big! The present can only be peace, can only be happiness.

WORRY

THE OLD WOMAN ON THE BUS

I have heard that an old woman was traveling on a bus, and she was anxious, worried, and continuously asking what stop it was.

The stranger sitting by her side said, "Relax, don't be worried. The conductor will go on announcing what stop it is, and if you are too worried I will call him here. You can tell him where you want to get off so he can keep a note of it. And you can relax!"

He called the conductor and the woman said, "Please remember, I don't want to miss my stop. I have to reach somewhere very urgently."

The conductor said, "Okay, I will make a note of it —although even without your asking I will be announcing each stop. But I will make a note of it and I will come to you particularly and tell you whenever your stop comes. But you relax, don't be so worried about it!"

She was perspiring and trembling and looked so tense. So she said, "Okay, you note it down—I have to get off at the bus terminus."

Now if it is the bus terminus, why should you worry? How can you miss it? There is no way of missing it!

The moment you rest, the moment you relax, you know that existence is already going, moving, reaching towards higher peaks. And you are part of it. You need not have separate ambitions. This is relaxation—resting, dropping all private goals, dropping the whole achieving mind, all the ego projections. And then life is a mystery. Your eyes will be full of wonder; your heart will be full of awe.

We are not to become something—we are already it. This is the whole message of all the awakened ones: that you are not to achieve something, it has already been given to you. It is God's gift. You are already where you should be, you can't be anywhere else. There is nowhere to go, nothing to achieve. Because there is nowhere to go and nothing to achieve, you can celebrate. Then there is no hurry, no worry, no anxiety, no anguish, no fear of being a failure. You can't fail. In the very nature of things it is impossible to fail, because there is no question of success at all.

Wishful Thinking

The thinker is creative with his thoughts — this is one of the most fundamental truths to be understood. All that you experience is your creation. First you create it, then you experience it, and then you are caught in the experience—because you don't know that the source of all exists in you.

Once a man was traveling, accidentally he entered paradise. In the Indian concept of paradise there are wishfulfilling trees, *kalpatarus.* You just sit underneath them, desire anything, and immediately it is fulfilled—there is no gap between the desire and its fulfillment. You think, and immediately it becomes a thing; the thought realizes automatically. These *kalpatarus* are nothing but symbolic for the mind. Mind is creative, creative with its thoughts.

Wishful Thinking

The Parable of the Wish-fulfilling Tree

The man was tired, so he fell asleep under a wish-fulfilling tree. When he woke up he was feeling very hungry, so he said, "I wish I could get some food from somewhere." And immediately food appeared out of nowhere—just floating in the air, delicious food. He immediately started eating, and when he was feeling very satisfied, another thought arose in him: "If only I could get something to drink..." And there is no prohibition in paradise so immediately, precious wine appeared.

Drinking the wine, relaxed in the cool breeze of paradise under the shade of the tree, he started wondering, "What is happening? Have I fallen into a dream, or are some ghosts around and playing tricks with me?" And ghosts appeared! They were ferocious, horrible, nauseating. He started trembling, and a thought arose in him: "Now I am sure to be killed. These people are going to kill me."

And he was killed.

This parable is an ancient parable, of immense significance. Your mind is the wish-fulfilling tree—whatsoever you think, sooner or later it is fulfilled. Sometimes the gap is such that you have completely forgotten that you had desired it in the first place—sometimes the gap is of years, or sometimes of lives, so you can't connect the source. But if you watch deeply you will find all your thoughts are creating you and your life. They create your hell, they create your heaven. They create your misery, they create your joy. They create the negative, they create the positive. Everybody is a magician, spinning and weaving a magic world around himself, and then he is caught—the spider itself is caught in its own web.

Once this is understood, things start changing. Then you can play around; then you can change your hell into heaven—it is just a question of painting it from a different vision. Or if you are so much in love with misery you can create as much as you want, to your heart's content. But then you are never complaining, because you know that it is your creation, it is your painting, you cannot make anybody feel responsible for it. Then the whole responsibility is yours.

Then a new possibility arises: you can drop creating the world, you can stop creating it. There is no need to create heaven and hell, there is no need to create at all. The creator can relax, retire.

That retirement of the mind is meditation.

Desire

When you desire something, your joy depends on that something. If it is taken away, you are miserable; if it is given to you, you are happy, but only for the moment. That too has to be understood. Whenever your desire is fulfilled it is only for the moment that you feel joy. It is fleeting, because once you have got it, again the mind starts desiring for more, for something else. Mind exists in desiring; hence mind can never leave you without desire. If you are without desire mind dies immediately. That's the whole secret of meditation.

A beggar knocks on the door of an emperor; it is early morning. The emperor was coming out for a morning walk in his beautiful garden; otherwise it would have been difficult for the beggar to have an appointment with him. But there was no mediator to prevent him.

The emperor said, "What do you want?"

Desire

The Magical Begging Bowl

The beggar said, "Before you ask that, think twice!"

The emperor has never seen such a lion of a man; he has fought wars, has won victories, has made it clear that nobody is more powerful than him, but suddenly this beggar says to him, "Think twice of what you are saying, because you may not be able to fulfill it!"

The king said, "Don't be worried, that is my concern; you ask what you want, it will be done!"

The beggar said, "You see my begging bowl? I want it to be filled! It does not matter with what, the only condition is that it should be filled, it should be full. You can still say no, but if you say yes, then you are taking a risk."

The emperor laughed. Just a beggar's bowl... and he is being given a warning? He told his premier to fill the beggar's bowl with diamonds, so that this beggar would know who he was asking. The beggar again said, "Think twice."

And soon it became apparent that the beggar was right, because the moment the diamonds were poured into his begging bowl they simply disappeared. The word began to spread like wildfire in the capital; thousands of people arrived to watch. When the precious stones were finished the king said, "Bring out all the gold and silver, everything! My whole kingdom, my whole integrity is being challenged." But by the evening everything had disappeared and there were only two beggars left—one used to be the emperor.

The emperor said, "Before I ask your forgiveness for not listening to your warning, please tell me the secret of this begging bowl."

The beggar said, "There is no secret. I have polished it, made it look like a bowl, but it is a human skull. You go on pouring anything into it and it disappears."

The story is tremendously meaningful. Have you ever thought about your own begging bowl? Everything disappears—power, prestige, respectability, riches—everything disappears and your begging bowl goes on opening its mouth for more. And the "more" takes you away from this. The desire, the longing for something else takes you away from this moment.

There are only two kinds of people in the world: the majority are running after shadows, their begging bowls will remain with them till they enter their graves. And a very small minority, one in a million, stops running, drops all desires, asks for nothing—and suddenly he finds everything within himself.

Living Totally

Those who say, "We are waiting for an opportunity," are being deceptive, and they are not deceiving anybody but themselves. The opportunity is not going to come tomorrow. It has already arrived, it has always been here. It was here even when you were not here. Existence is an opportunity; to be is the opportunity.

Don't say, "Tomorrow I will meditate, tomorrow I will love, tomorrow I will have a dancing relationship with existence." Why tomorrow? Tomorrow never comes. Why not now? Why postpone? Postponement is a trick of the mind; it keeps you hoping, and meanwhile the opportunity is slipping by. And in the end you will come to the cul-de-sac—death—and there will be no more opportunity left. And this has happened many times in the past. You are not new here, you have been born and you have died many, many times. And each time the mind has played the same trick, and you have not yet learned anything.

Living Totally

Alexander the Great Meets Diogenes

When Alexander the Great was coming to India, he met one strange man, Diogenes. It was a winter morning, a cool breeze was blowing, and Diogenes was lying on the riverbank, taking a sun-bath, naked. He was a beautiful man. When there is a beautiful soul, a beauty arises which is not of this world.

He had nothing, not even a begging-bowl, because one day when he was going toward the river with his begging bowl to get some water to drink, he saw a dog rushing to the river. The dog jumped in the river and drank—Diogenes laughed and he said, "This dog has taught me a lesson. If he can live without a begging bowl, then why can't I?" He threw the begging-bowl, he also jumped like the dog in the river and drank. Since then he had had nothing.

Alexander had never seen such a graceful man, such utter beauty, something from the unknown…. He was in awe and he said, "Sir..." He had not said "Sir" to anybody in his life. He said, "Sir, I am immensely impressed by your being, and I would like to do something for you. Is there something that I can do for you?

Diogenes said, "Just stand to the side because you are blocking the sun—that's all. Nothing else do I need."

Alexander said, "If I have another chance to come to the earth I will ask God, instead of making me Alexander again, to make me Diogenes."

Diogenes laughed and he said, "Who is preventing you right now? You can become a Diogenes. Where are you going? For months I have seen armies moving and moving—where are you going? and for what?"

Alexander said, I am going to India to conquer the whole world."

"And then what are you going to do?" Diogenes asked.

And Alexander said, "Then I will rest."

Diogenes laughed again and he said, "You are mad —because I am resting now, and I have not conquered the world. I don't see the necessity of it. Who has told you that before resting, you have to conquer the world? And I tell you: if you don't rest now, then you never will. Something or other will always remain to be conquered... and time is fleeting. You will die in the middle of your journey—everybody dies in the middle of the journey."

And Alexander died in the middle. When he was moving back from India, he died on the way. And that day he remembered Diogenes. Only Diogenes was in his mind—he could never rest in his life, and that man rested.

The Quest

Gather all courage and take a jump. You will still exist, but in such a new way that you cannot connect it with the old. It will be a discontinuity. The old was so tiny, so small, so mean, and the new is so vast. From a small dewdrop you have become the ocean. But even the dewdrop slipping from a lotus leaf trembles for a moment, tries to hang on a little more, because he can see the ocean... once he has fallen from the lotus leaf he is gone. Yes, in a way he will not be; as a dewdrop he will be gone. But it is not a loss. He will be oceanic.

And all other oceans are limited. The ocean of existence is unlimited.

THE QUEST

SEARCHING FOR THE HOUSE OF GOD

I have talked many times about a beautiful poem of Rabindranath Tagore. The poet has been searching for God for millions of lives. He has seen him sometimes, far away, near a star, and he started moving that way, but by the time he reached that star, God has moved to some other place. But he went on searching and searching—he was determined to find God's home—and the surprise of surprises was, one day he actually reached a house where on the door was written: "God's Home."

You can understand his ecstasy, you can understand his joy. He runs up the steps, and just as he is going to knock on the door, suddenly his hand freezes. An idea arises in him: "If by chance this is really the home of God, then I am finished, my seeking is finished. I have become identified with my seeking, with my search. I don't know anything else. If the door opens and I face God, I am finished—the search is over. Then what?"

He starts trembling with fear, takes his shoes off his feet, and descends back down the beautiful marble steps. His fear is that God may open the door, although he has not knocked. And then he runs as fast as he has never run before. He used to think that he had been running after God as fast as he could, but today he runs as he has never run, not looking back.

The poem ends, "I am still searching for God. I know his home, so I avoid it and search everywhere else. The excitement is great, the challenge is great, and in my search I continue to exist. God is a danger—I will be annihilated. But now I am not afraid even of God, because I know where he lives. So, leaving his home aside, I go on searching for him all around the universe. And deep down I know my search is not for God; my search is to nourish my ego."

Rabindranath Tagore is not ordinarily associated with religion. But only a religious man of tremendous experience can write this poem. It is not just ordinary poetry; it contains such a great truth.

This is the situation: blissfulness does not allow you to exist; you have to disappear. That's why you don't see many blissful people in the world. Misery nourishes your ego—that's why you see so many miserable people in the world. The basic, central point is the ego.

For the realization of ultimate truth, you have to pay the price—and the price is nothing but dropping the ego. So when such a moment comes, don't hesitate. Dancingly, disappear... with a great laughter, disappear; with songs on your lips, disappear.

Hope

The joy of love is possible only if you have known the joy of being alone, because then only do you have something to share. Otherwise, two beggars meeting each other, clinging to each other, cannot be blissful. They will create misery for each other because each will be hoping, and hoping in vain, that "The other is going to fulfill me." The other is hoping the same. They cannot fulfill each other. They are both blind; they cannot help each other.

Hope

Lost in the jungle

I have heard about a hunter who got lost in the jungle. For three days he could not find anybody to ask for the way out, and he was becoming more and more panicky—three days of no food and three days of constant fear of wild animals. For three days he was not able to sleep; he was sitting awake on some tree, afraid he may be attacked. There were snakes, there were lions, there were wild animals. On the fourth day early in the morning, he saw a man sitting under a tree. You can imagine his joy. He rushed, he hugged the man, and he said, "What joy!" And the other man hugged him, and both were immensely happy. Then they asked each other, "Why are you so ecstatic?" The first said, "I was lost and I was waiting to meet somebody." And the other said, "I am also lost and I am waiting to meet somebody. But if we are both lost then the ecstasy is just foolish. So now we will be lost together!"

That's what happens: you are lonely, the other is lonely—now you meet. First the honeymoon: that ecstasy that you have met the other, now you will not be lonely any more. But within three days, or if you are intelligent enough, then within three hours... it depends on how intelligent you are. If you are stupid, then it will take a longer time because one does not learn; otherwise the intelligent person can immediately see after three minutes... "What are we trying to do? It is not going to happen. The other is as lonely as I am. Now we will be living together—two lonelinesses together. Two wounds together cannot help each other to be healed."

We are part of each other—no man is an island. We belong to an invisible but infinite continent. Boundless is our existence.

But those experiences happen only to people who are self-actualizing, who are in such tremendous love with themselves that they can close their eyes and be alone and be utterly blissful. That's what meditation is all about.

Meditation means being ecstatic in your aloneness. But when you become ecstatic in your aloneness, soon the ecstasy is so much that you cannot contain it. It starts overflowing you. And when it starts overflowing you it becomes love. Meditation allows love to happen. And the people who have not known meditation will never know love. They may pretend that they love but they cannot. They will only pretend—because they don't have anything to give, they are not overflowing.

Love is a sharing. But before you can share, you have to have it! Meditation should be the first thing. Meditation is the center, love is the circumference of it. Meditation is the flame, love is the radiation of it. Meditation is the flower, love is the fragrance of it.

Challenge

Misery only means that things are not fitting with your desires—and things never fit with your desires, they cannot. Things simply go on following their nature.

Lao Tzu calls this nature Tao. Buddha calls this nature Dhamma. Mahavir has defined religion as "the nature of things." Nothing can be done. Fire is hot and water is cool. The wise man is one who relaxes with the nature of things, who follows the nature of things.

And when you follow the nature of things, no shadow is cast. There is no misery. Even sadness is luminous then, even sadness has a beauty then. Not that sadness will not come—it will come, but it will not be your enemy. You will befriend it, because you will see its necessity. You will be able to see its grace, and you will be able to see why it is there and why it is needed.

Challenge

The Parable of the Farmer and the Wheat

I have heard an ancient parable—it must be very ancient, because God used to live on the earth in those days. One day a man came to him, an old farmer, and he said, "Look, you may be God, and you may have created the world, but one thing I must say to you: you are not a farmer. You don't know even the ABC of farming. You have something to learn."

God said, "What's your advice?"

The farmer said, "You give me one year's time, and just let things be according to me, and see what happens. There will be no poverty left!"

God was willing, and one year was given to the farmer. Naturally, he asked for the best, he thought only of the best—no thunder, no strong winds, no dangers for the crop. Everything was comfortable, cozy, and he was very happy. The wheat was growing so high! When he wanted sun, there was sun; when he wanted rain, there was rain, and as much as he wanted. This year everything was right, mathematically right.

But when the crops were harvested, there was no wheat inside. The farmer was surprised. He asked God, "What happened? What went wrong?"

God said, "Because there was no challenge, because there was no conflict, no friction, because you avoided all that was bad, the wheat remained impotent. A little struggle is a must. Storms are needed, thunder, lightning is needed. They shake up the soul inside the wheat."

This parable is of immense value. If you are just happy and happy and happy, happiness will lose all meaning. It will be as if somebody is writing with white chalk on a white wall. Nobody will ever be able to read it. You have to write on a black board, then it comes clear . The night is as much needed as the day. And the days of sadness are as essential as the days of happiness.

This I call understanding. Once you understand it, you relax—in that relaxation is surrender. You say, "Thy will be done." You say, "Do whatsoever you feel is right. If today clouds are needed, give me clouds. Don't listen to me, my understanding is tiny. What do I know of life and its secrets? Don't listen to me! You just go on doing your will."

And, slowly slowly, the more you see the rhythm of life, the rhythm of duality, the rhythm of polarity, you stop asking, you stop choosing.

This is the secret. Live with this secret, and see the beauty. Live with this secret, and you will be suddenly surprised: How great is the blessing of life! How much is being showered on you every moment!

Love

The seed is never in danger, remember. What danger can there be for the seed? It is absolutely protected. But the plant is always in danger, the plant is very soft. The seed is like a stone, hard, hidden behind a hard crust. But the plant has to pass through a thousand and one hazards. And not all plants are going to attain to that height where they can bloom into flowers, a thousand and one flowers.... Very few human beings attain to the second stage, and very few of those who attain the second stage attain the third, the stage of the flower. Why can't they attain the third stage, the stage of the flower? Because of greed, because of miserliness, they are not ready to share... because of a state of unlovingness. Courage is needed to become a plant, and love is needed to become a flower. A flower means the tree is opening up its heart, releasing its perfume, giving its soul, pouring its being into existence. Don't remain a seed. Gather courage—courage to drop the ego, courage to drop the securities, courage to drop the safeties, courage to be vulnerable.

Love

The King's Challenge to His Three Sons

A great king had three sons, and he wanted to choose one to be his heir. It was very difficult, because all three were very intelligent, very courageous. Whom should he choose? So he asked a great sage, and the sage suggested an idea....

The king went home and he asked all the three sons to come together. He gave them each one bag of flower seeds, and told them that he was going for a pilgrimage. "It will take a few years—one, two, three, maybe more. And this is a kind of test for you. These seeds you will have to give back to me when I return. Whosoever protects them best will become my heir." And he left for the pilgrimage.

The first son locked them in an iron safe—because when the father comes he has to return them as they are.

The second son thought, "If I lock them up just as my brother has done, these seeds will die. And a dead seed is not a seed at all. And my father may argue that "I had given you live seeds, there was a possibility for them to grow—but these seeds are dead; they cannot grow." So he went into the market and sold the seeds and kept the money. And he thought, "When my father comes I will go to the market, purchase new seeds, and give him back better than the first."

But the third was the best. He went back into the garden and threw the seeds all over the place.

After three years, when the father came back, the first son opened his safe. Those seeds were all dead, stinking. And the father said, "What! These are the seeds I have given to you? They had the possibility to bloom into flowers and give great perfume—and these seeds are stinking. These are not my seeds!"

He went to the second son. He rushed to the market, purchased seeds, came back home, and said, "These are the seeds." The father said, "You are better than the first, but yet not as capable as I would like you to be."

He went to the third. With great hope, and fear too: "What has he done?" And the third took him back into the garden and there were millions of plants blooming, millions of flowers all around. And the son said, "These are the seeds you had given to me. Soon I will collect the seeds and give them back to you. Right now they are getting ready to be collected."

The father said, "You are my heir. This is how one should behave with seeds."

Compassion

People come to me and they ask, "What is right and what is wrong?" I say, "Awareness is right; unawareness is wrong." I don't label actions as wrong and right. I don't say violence is wrong. Sometimes violence can be right. I don't say love is right. Sometimes love can be wrong. Love can be for a wrong person, love can be for a wrong purpose. Somebody loves his country. Now, this is wrong because nationalism is a curse. Somebody loves his religion. He can kill, he can murder, he can burn others' temples. Neither is love always right nor is anger always wrong.

Then what is right and what is wrong? To me, awareness is right. If you are angry with full awareness, even anger is right. And if you are loving with unawareness, even love is not right. So let the quality of awareness be there in every act that you do, in every thought that you think, in every dream that you dream. Let the quality of awareness enter into your being more and more. Become suffused with the quality of awareness. Then whatsoever you do is virtue. Then whatsoever you do is good. Then whatsoever you do is a blessing to you and to the world in which you live.

Compassion

Jesus and the Money-Changers

Let me remind you of a situation that happened in Jesus' life. He took a whip and entered into the great temple of Jerusalem. A whip in the hand of Jesus...? This is what Buddha means when he says, "an unwounded hand can handle poison." Yes, Jesus can handle a whip, no problem; the whip cannot overpower him. He remains alert, his consciousness is such.

The great temple of Jerusalem had become a place of robbers. There were money-changers inside the temple and they were exploiting the whole country. Jesus alone entered the temple and upturned their boards—the boards of the money-changers—threw their money around and created such turmoil that the money-changers escaped outside the temple. They were many and Jesus was alone, but he was in such a fury, in such a fire!

Now, this has been a problem for the Christians: how to explain it?—because their whole effort is to prove that Jesus is a dove, a symbol of peace. How can he take a whip in his hands? How can he be so angry, so enraged, that he upturned the boards of the money-changers and threw them outside the temple? And he must have been afire; otherwise, he was alone—he could have been caught hold of.

His energy must have been in a storm; they could not face him. The priests and the business people all escaped outside shouting, "This man has gone mad!"

Christians avoid this story. There is no need to avoid it if you understand: Jesus is so innocent! He is not angry; it is his compassion. He is not violent, he is not destructive; it is his love. The whip in his hand is the whip in the hands of love, compassion.

A man of awareness acts out of his awareness, hence there is no repentance; his action is total. And one of the beauties of the total action is that it does not create karma; it does not create anything; it doesn't leave any trace on you. It is like writing on water: you have not even finished... it is gone. It is not even writing in sand, because that may remain for a few hours if the wind does not come—it is writing on water.

If you can be totally alert, then there is no problem. You can handle poison; then the poison will function as a medicine. In the hands of the wise, poison becomes medicine; in the hands of the fools, even medicine, even nectar, is bound to become poison. If you function out of innocence—not out of knowledgeability but out of childlike innocence—then you can never come to any harm, because it leaves no trace. You remain free of your actions. You live totally and yet no action burdens you.

Dropping the Past

Gather courage—the journey has already started. Even if you go back you will not find the old shore again. Even if you go back, those old toys will not be of any help anymore; you are finished with them, you will know they are toys. Now the real has to be found, has to be inquired into. And it is not very far away either—it is within you.

Dropping the Past

"Let the Dead Bury the Dead"

A man who lives according to the past is bound to feel boredom, meaninglessness, and a kind of anguish: "What am I doing here? Why am I continuing to live? What is there in tomorrow?—another repetition of today? And what was in today was a repetition of yesterday." So what is the point? Why go dragging yourself from the cradle to the grave, in the same routine?

It is perfectly good for buffaloes and donkeys because they don't have a memory of the past, they don't have any idea of the future. They are not bored, because for boredom a certain consciousness is needed. This consciousness is aware that you have done it before, you are doing it again, and you will be doing it tomorrow also—because you don't move from the past, you don't let it die, you keep it alive. This is the dilemma that everybody faces in life, and the only solution is to let the past die.

There is a beautiful story in the life of Jesus. He comes to a lake; it is early morning, the sun has yet not risen, and one fisherman is just going to throw his net into the lake. Jesus puts his hand on his shoulder and says, "How long are you going to do this thing, every day—morning, afternoon, evening—just catching fish? Do you think this is all life is meant for?"

The fisherman says, "I have never thought about it, but because you have raised the question, I can see the point, that life must be something more."

Jesus says, "If you come with me I will teach you how to catch men, rather than catching fish." The man looked into Jesus' eyes... such depth, such sincerity, so much love that you cannot doubt this man, such a great silence surrounding him that you cannot say no to this man. The fisherman threw his net into the water and followed Jesus.

As they were leaving the town a man came running and told the fisherman, "Your father who was ill for many days has died. Come home!"

The fisherman asked Jesus, "Just give me three days so that I can do the last rituals that a son is expected to do when his father dies."

And this is the statement that I want you to remember: Jesus said to that fisherman, "Let the dead bury their dead, you come with me."

What does he mean? "The whole city is full of dead people; they will manage to dispose of your dead father. You are not needed. You just come with me."

Every moment something is becoming dead. Don't be antique collectors; that which is dead, leave it. You go with life, you flow with life, with your totality and intensity, and you will never face any dilemma, any problem.

Repentance

If you have done something wrong, go to the person. Be humble, ask his forgiveness. Only he can forgive you, nobody else. And remember, that is the meaning of the word "sin": forgetfulness. So now, don't forget again and do the same; otherwise, your asking forgiveness becomes meaningless. Now be careful, be alert, be conscious; and don't do the same thing again. Remember not to commit the mistake again—it should become a decision in you; then you are really repentant.

Repentance can become a very, very deep phenomenon in you if you understand the responsibility. Then even a small thing, if it becomes a repentance—not just verbal, not just on the surface; if it goes deep to your roots, if you repent from the roots; if your whole being shakes and trembles and cries, and tears come out; not only out of your eyes, but out of every cell of your body, then repentance can become a transfiguration.

Repentance

When Shibli Threw the Rose

The first time Shibli's name became known was the time when Mansoor al-Hillaj was being murdered. Many people have been murdered in the past by so called religious people—Jesus was murdered—but there has been never such a murder as happened with al-Hillaj. First his legs were cut off—he was alive—then his hands were cut. Then his tongue was cut, then his eyes were taken out—and he was alive. He was cut in pieces. And what crime had Mansoor committed? He had said, "*An'al Hak.*" It means "I am the Truth, I am God." All the seers of the Upanishads declare this, "*Aham Brahmasmi*—I am Brahma, the Supreme Self." But the Mohammedans could not tolerate it.

Mansoor is one of the greatest Sufis. When they started cutting his hands he looked at the sky, prayed to God and said, "You cannot deceive me! I can see you in everybody present here. You are trying to deceive me? you have come as the murderer? as the enemy? But I tell you, in whatsoever form you come I will recognize you—because I have recognized you within myself. Now there is no possibility of deception."

Shibli was a companion, a friend to al-Hillaj. People are throwing stones and mud in ridicule, and Shibli is standing there. Mansoor is laughing and smiling. Suddenly he starts crying and weeping, because Shibli has thrown a rose at him. Somebody asked, "What is the matter? With stones you laugh—have you gone mad? And Shibli has thrown only a rose flower. Why are you crying and weeping?"

Mansoor said, "People who are throwing stones don't know what they are doing, but this Shibli has to know. For him it will be difficult to get forgiveness from God." He said, "Others will be forgiven because they are acting in ignorance; they cannot help it. In their blindness that's all they can do. But with Shibli—a man who knows! That's why I weep and cry for him. He is the only person who is committing a sin here."

And this statement of Mansoor's changed Shibli completely. He threw the Koran, the scriptures, and he said, "They could not make me understand even this: that all knowledge is useless. Now I will seek the right knowledge." And later on when he was asked, "Why did you throw the flower?" Shibli said, "I was afraid of the crowd—if I don't throw anything, people may think that I belong to Mansoor's group. They may get violent toward me. I threw the flower—just a compromise. Mansoor was right: he wept at my fear, my cowardice. He wept because I was compromising with the crowd." But Shibli understood. The crying of Mansoor became a transformation.

Play

Your mind goes on playing infinitely—the whole thing is just like a dream in an empty room. While meditating, one has to look at the mind just frolicking, just like children playing and jumping out of overflowing energy, that's all. Thoughts jumping, frolicking, just a play—don't be serious about them. Even if a bad thought is there, don't feel guilty. Or, if there is a very great thought, a very good thought—that you want to serve humanity and transform the whole world, and you want to bring heaven onto earth—don't get too much ego through it, don't feel that you have become great. This is just a frolicking mind. Sometimes it goes down, sometimes it comes up—it is just overflowing energy, taking many shapes and forms.

Play

Krishna's Challenge to Arjuna

The dimension of play has to be applied to your whole life. Whatsoever you are doing, be there in that activity so totally that the end is irrelevant. The end will come, it has to come, but it is not on your mind. You are playing, you are enjoying.

That's what Krishna means—during the Mahabharata, the great war that is chronicled in the *Gita*—when he tells his disciple Arjuna to leave the future in the hands of the Divine: "The result of your activity is in the hands of the Divine, you simply do." This "simply doing" becomes a play. That's what Arjuna finds difficult to understand, because he says that if it is just play then why kill, why fight? But Krishna's whole life is just a play; you cannot find such a non-serious man anywhere. His whole life is just a play, a game, a drama. He is enjoying everything but he is not serious about it. He is enjoying it intensely but he is not worried about the result. What happens is irrelevant.

It is difficult for Arjuna to understand Krishna because Arjuna calculates, he thinks in terms of the end result. He says in the beginning of the *Gita*, "This whole thing seems to be absurd. On both sides my friends and my relatives are standing to fight. Whosoever wins, it will be a loss because my family, my relatives, my friends will be destroyed. Even if I win, it will not be worth anything because to whom am I going to show my victory? Victories are meaningful because friends, relatives, family will enjoy them. But there will be no one, the victory will be just over dead bodies. Who will appreciate it? Who will say, 'Arjuna, you have done a great deed'? So whether I am victorious or I am defeated, it seems absurd. The whole thing is nonsense." He wants to renounce. He is deadly serious, and anyone who calculates will be that deadly serious.

The setting of the *Gita* is unique. War is the most serious affair. You cannot be playful about it, because lives are involved, millions of lives are involved—you cannot be playful. And Krishna insists that even there you have to be playful. You don't think about what will happen in the end, you just be here and now. You just be a warrior, playing. Don't get worried about the result because the result is in the hands of the Divine. And it is not even the point if the result is in the hands of the Divine or not—the point is that it should not be in your hands, you should not carry it. If you carry it then your life cannot become meditative.

Single-Pointedness

Mind is so cunning that it can hide in the garments of its very opposite. From indulgence it can become asceticism, from being a materialist it can become a spiritualist, from being worldly it can become otherworldly. But mind is mind—whether you are for the world or against the world you remain encaged in the mind. For or against, both are parts of the mind.

When mind disappears, mind disappears in a choiceless awareness. When you stop choosing, when you are neither for nor against—that is stopping in the middle. One choice leads to the left, one extreme; another choice leads to the right, the other extreme. If you don't choose, you are exactly in the middle. That is relaxation, that is rest. You become choiceless, unobsessed, and in that state of unobsessed, choiceless consciousness, intelligence arises which has been lying deep, dormant in your being. You become a light unto yourself.

Single-Pointedness

Saraha and the Arrowsmith Woman

Saraha, the founder of Tantra, was the son of a very learned Brahmin who was in the court of King Mahapala. The king was willing to give his own daughter to Saraha, but Saraha wanted to renounce all— he wanted to become a sannyasin. The king tried to persuade him—Saraha was so beautiful and he was so intelligent and he was such a handsome young man. But he persisted and the permission had to be given—Saraha became a disciple of Sri Kirti.

The first thing Sri Kirti told him was: "Forget all your Vedas and all your learning and all that nonsense." It was difficult but he was ready to stake anything. Years passed and, by and by, he erased all that he had known. He became a great meditator.

One day while Saraha was meditating, suddenly he saw a vision—that there was a woman in the marketplace who was going to be his real teacher. He went to the marketplace. He saw this woman, young woman, very alive, radiant with life, cutting an arrow-shaft, looking neither to the right nor to the left, but wholly absorbed in making the arrow. He immediately felt something extraordinary in her presence, something that he had never come across. Something so fresh and something from the very source. The arrow ready, the woman closing one eye and opening the other, assumed the posture of aiming at an invisible target...

And something happened, something like a communion. Saraha had never felt like that before. In that moment, the spiritual significance of what she was doing dawned upon him. Neither looking to the left, nor looking to the right—just looking in the middle.

For the first time he understood what Buddha means by being in the middle: avoid the axis. You can move from the left to the right, from the right to the left, but you will be like a pendulum moving. To be in the middle means the pendulum just hangs there, neither to the right nor to the left. Then the clock stops, then the world stops. Then there is no more time... then the state of no-time.

He had heard it said so many times by Sri Kirti; he had read about it, he had pondered, contemplated over it; he had argued with others about it, that to be in the middle is the right thing. For the first time he had seen it in an action: the woman was not looking to the right and not looking to the left... she was just looking in the middle, focussed in the middle.

The middle is the point from where the transcendence happens. Think about it, contemplate about it, watch it in life.

Sex

Sex holds great secrets in it, and the first secret is—if you meditate you will see it—that joy comes because sex disappears. And whenever you are in that moment of joy, time also disappears—if you meditate on it—the mind also disappears. And these are the qualities of meditation.

My own observation is that the first glimpse of meditation in the world must have come through sex; there is no other way. Meditation must have entered into life through sex, because this is the most meditative phenomenon—if you understand it, if you go deep into it, if you just don't use it like a drug. Then slowly, slowly, as more understanding grows, the hankering disappears, and one day comes of great freedom when sex no more haunts you. Then one is quiet, silent, utterly oneself. The need for the other has disappeared. One can still make love if one chooses to, but there is no need. Then it will be a kind of sharing.

Sex

The Circle of Mahamudra

When two lovers are in deep sexual orgasm, they melt into each other; then the woman is no longer the woman, the man is no longer the man. They become just like the circle of yin and yang, reaching into each other, meeting in each other, melting, their own identities forgotten. That's why love is so beautiful. This state is called *mudra;* this state of deep orgasmic intercourse is called *mudra.* And the final state of orgasm with the whole is called *Mahamudra,* the great orgasm.

Orgasm is a state where your body no longer is felt as matter; it vibrates like energy, electricity. It vibrates so deeply, from the very foundation, that you completely forget that it is a material thing. It becomes an electric phenomenon—and it is an electric phenomenon. Now physicists say that there is no matter, that all matter is only appearance; deep down, that which exists is electricity, not matter. In orgasm, you come to this deepest layer of your body where matter no longer exists, just energy waves; you become a dancing energy, vibrating. No more any boundaries to you—pulsating, but no longer substantial. And your beloved also pulsates.

And by and by, if the partners love each other and they surrender to each other, they surrender to this moment of pulsation, of vibration, of being energy, and they are not scared....

Because it is death-like when the body loses boundaries, when the body becomes like a vaporous thing, when the body evaporates substantially and only energy is left, a very subtle rhythm, but you find yourself as if you are not. Only in deep love can one move into it. Love is like death: you die as far as your material image is concerned, you die as far as you think you are a body; you die as a body and you evolve as energy, vital energy.

And when the wife and the husband, or the lovers, or the partners, start vibrating in a rhythm, their heartbeats and their bodies come together, it becomes a harmony—then orgasm happens, then they are no longer two. That is the symbol of yin and yang: yin moving into yang, yang moving into yin; man moving into the woman, the woman moving into the man. Now they are a circle and they vibrate together, they pulsate together. Their hearts are no longer separate, their beats are no longer separate; they have become a melody, a harmony. It is the greatest music possible; all other musics are just faint things compared to it, shadow things compared to it.

This vibration of two as one is orgasm. When the same thing happens, not with another person, but with the whole existence, then it is *Mahamudra,* then it is the great orgasm.

Devotion

Devotion is a way of merging and melting into existence. It is not a pilgrimage; it is simply losing all the boundaries that divide you from existence—it is a love affair.

Love is a merger with an individual, a deep intimacy of two hearts—so deep that the two hearts start dancing in the same harmony. Although the hearts are two, the harmony is one, the music is one, the dance is one. What love is between individuals, devotion is between one individual and the whole existence. He dances in the waves of the ocean, he dances in the dancing trees in the sun, he dances with the stars. His heart responds to the fragrance of the flowers, to the song of the birds, to the silences of the night. Devotion is the death of the personality. That which is mortal in you, you drop of your own accord; only the immortal remains, the eternal remains, the deathless remains. And naturally the deathless cannot be separate from existence—which is deathless, which is always ongoing, knows no beginning, no end.

Devotion is the highest form of love.

Devotion

Meera's Temple Dance

You know Jesus said, "God is love." If it had been written by a woman she would have written, "Love is God." God must be secondary; it is a mental hypothesis. But love is a reality throbbing in every heart.

We have seen people like Meera.... But only very courageous women could manage to come out of the repressive social system. She could manage because she was a queen, although her own family tried to kill her because she was dancing on the streets, singing songs. The family could not tolerate it. Particularly in India, and in Rajasthan, the woman is very much repressed. And a woman of the beauty of Meera, dancing in the streets, singing songs of joy...

There was a temple in Vrindavan, where Krishna had resided. In his memory a great temple was made, and in that temple, no woman was allowed to enter. Women were allowed only on the outside, to touch the steps of the temple. They never saw the statue of Krishna inside, because the priest was very adamant. When Meera came the priest was afraid that she would enter the temple.

Two men with swords, naked swords, were placed before the gate to prevent Meera from coming in. But when she came—and such people are so rare, such a fragrant breeze, such a beautiful dance, such a song that brings into words that which cannot be brought into words—those two swordsmen forgot why they were standing there and Meera danced into the temple. It was the time for the priest to worship Krishna. His plate, full of flowers, fell onto the ground as he saw Meera.

He was utterly angry and he said to Meera, "You have broken a rule of hundreds of years."

She said, "What rule?"

The priest said, "No woman can enter here."

And can you believe the answer? This is courage... Meera said, "Then how have you entered here? Except one, the ultimate, the beloved, everybody is a woman. Do you think there are two men in the world—you and the ultimate? Forget all this nonsense." Certainly she was right. A woman full of heart looks at existence as a beloved. And existence is one.

INTELLIGENCE

We are born to be blissful, it is our birthright. But people are so foolish, they don't even claim their birthright. They become more interested in what others possess and they start running after those things. They never look within, they never search in their own house.

The intelligent person will begin his search from his inner being—that will be his first exploration—because unless I know what is within me how can I go on searching all over the world?—it is such a vast world. And those who have looked within have found it instantly, immediately. It is not a question of gradual progress, it is a sudden phenomenon, a sudden enlightenment.

Intelligence

Rabia and the Riddle of the Lost Needle

I have heard about a very great Sufi mystic woman, Rabia al-Adawia.

One evening, people found her sitting on the road searching for something. She was an old woman, her eyes were weak, and it was difficult for her to see. So the neighbors came to help her.

They asked, "What are you searching for?"

Rabia said, "That question is irrelevant, I am searching. If you can help me, help."

They laughed and said, "Rabia, have you gone mad? You say our question is irrelevant, but if we don't know what you are searching for, how can we help?"

Rabia said, "Okay. Just to satisfy you, I am searching for my needle, I have lost my needle."

They started helping her—but immediately they became aware of the fact that the road was very big and a needle was a very tiny thing.

So they asked Rabia, "Please tell us where you lost it—the exact, precise place. Otherwise it is difficult. The road is big and we can go on searching and searching forever. Where did you lose it?"

Rabia said, "Again you ask an irrelevant question. How is it concerned with my search?"

They stopped. They said, "You have certainly gone crazy!"

Rabia said, "Okay. Just to satisfy you, I have lost it in my house."

They asked, "Then why are you searching here?"

And Rabia is reported to have said, "Because here there is light and there is no light inside."

The sun was setting and there was a little light still left on the road.

This parable is very significant. Have you ever asked yourself what you are searching for? Have you ever made it a point of deep meditation to know what you are searching for? No. Even if in some vague moments, dreaming moments, you have some inkling of what you are searching for, it is never precise, it is never exact. You have not yet defined it. If you try to define it, the more it becomes defined the more you will feel that there is no need to search for it. The search can continue only in a state of vagueness, in a state of dreaming; when things are not clear you simply go on searching. Pulled by some inner urge, pushed by some inner urgency, one thing you do know: you need to search. This is an inner need. But you don't know what you are seeking.

And unless you know what you are seeking, how can you find it? It is vague—you think it is in money, power, prestige, respectability. But then you see people who are respectable, people who are powerful—they are

INTELLIGENCE

also seeking. Then you see people who are tremendously rich—they are also seeking. To the very end of their life they are seeking. So richness is not going to help, power is not going to help. The search continues in spite of what you have.

The search must be for something else. These names, these labels—money, power, prestige—these are just to satisfy your mind. They are just to help you feel that you are searching for something. That something is still undefined, a very vague feeling.

The first thing for the real seeker, for the seeker who has become a little alert, aware, is to define the search; to formulate a clear-cut concept of it, what it is; to bring it out of the dreaming consciousness; to look into it directly; to face it. Immediately a transformation starts happening. If you start defining your search, you will start losing your interest in the search. The more defined it becomes, the less it is there. Once it is clearly known what it is, suddenly it disappears. It exists only when you are not attentive.

Let it be repeated: the search exists only when you are sleepy; the search exists only when you are not aware. The unawareness creates the search.

Yes, Rabia is right. Inside there is no light. And because there is no light and no consciousness inside, of course you go on searching outside—because outside it seems more clear.

Our senses are all extroverted. The eyes open outwards, the hands move, spread outwards, the legs move into the outside, the ears listen to the outside noises, sounds. Whatsoever is available to you is all opening towards the outside; all the five senses move in an extrovert way. You start searching there where you see, feel, touch—the light of the senses falls outside. And the seeker is inside.

This dichotomy has to be understood. The seeker is inside but because the light is outside, the seeker starts moving in an ambitious way, trying to find something outside which will be fulfilling.

It is never going to happen. It has never happened. It cannot happen in the nature of things—because, unless you have sought the seeker, all your search is meaningless. Unless you come to know who you are, all that you seek is futile, because you don't know the seeker. Without knowing the seeker how can you move in the right dimension, in the right direction? It is impossible. The first things should be considered first.

If all seeking has stopped and you have suddenly become aware that now there is only one thing to know - "Who is this seeker in me? What is this energy that wants

INTELLIGENCE

to seek? Who am I?"—then there is a transformation. All values change suddenly. You start moving inwards.

Then Rabia is no longer sitting on the road searching for a needle that is lost somewhere in the darkness of one's own inner soul. Once you have started moving inwards.... In the beginning it is very dark—Rabia is right. It is very, very dark because for lives together you have never been inside—your eyes have been focussed on the outside world.

Have you watched it? Sometimes when you come in from the road where it is very sunny and there is bright light—when you suddenly come into the house it is very dark because the eyes are focussed for the outside light. When there is much light, the pupils of the eyes shrink. In darkness the eyes have to relax. But if you sit a little while, by and by the darkness disappears. There is more light; your eyes are settling.

For many lives you have been outside in the hot sun, in the world, so when you go in you have completely forgotten how to re-adjust your eyes. Meditation is nothing but a re-adjustment of your vision, of your eyes. And if you go on looking inside—it takes time—gradually, slowly, you start feeling a beautiful light inside. But it is not aggressive light; it is not like the sun, it is more like the moon. It is not glaring, it is not dazzling, it is very cool; it is not hot, it is very compassionate, it is very soothing, it is a balm.

By and by, when you have adjusted to the inside light, you will see that you are the very source. The seeker is the sought. Then you will see that the treasure is within you and the whole problem was that you were seeking for it outside. You were seeking for it somewhere outside and it has always been here within you. You were seeking in a wrong direction, that's all.

Doing

Each day it happens: you could have done something but you didn't do it, and you are using the excuse that if God wants it done, He will do it anyhow. Or, you do something and then you wait for the result, you expect, and the result never comes. Then you are angry, as if you have been cheated, as if God has betrayed you, as if He is against you, partial, prejudiced, unjust. And there arises great complaint in your mind. Then trust is missing.

The religious person is one who goes on doing whatsoever is humanly possible but creates no tension because of it. Because we are very, very tiny, small atoms in this universe, things are very complicated. Nothing depends only on my action; there are thousands of crisscrossing energies. The total of the energies will decide the outcome. How can I decide the outcome? But if I don't do anything then things may never be the same. I have to do, and yet I have to learn not to expect. Then doing is a kind of prayer, with no desire that the result should be such. Then there is no frustration. Trust will help you to remain unfrustrated, and tethering the camel will help you to remain alive, intensely alive.

Doing

Trust in Allah, But Tether Your Camel First

This Sufi saying wants to create the third type of man, the real man: who knows how to do and who knows how not to do; who can be a doer when needed, can say "Yes!", and who can be passive when needed and can say "No"; who is utterly wakeful in the day and utterly asleep in the night; who knows how to inhale and how to exhale; who knows the balance of life.

"Trust in Allah but tether your camel first." This saying comes from a small story.

A master was traveling with one of his disciples. The disciple was in charge of taking care of the camel. They came in the night, tired, to a caravanserai. It was the disciple's duty to tether the camel; he didn't bother about it, he left the camel outside. Instead of that he simply prayed. He said to God, "Take care of the camel," and fell asleep.

In the morning the camel was gone—stolen or moved away, or whatsoever happened. The master asked, "What happened to the camel? Where is the camel?"

And the disciple said, "I don't know. You ask God, because I had told Allah to take care of the camel, and I was too tired, so I don't know. And I am not responsible either, because I had told Him, and very clearly! There was no missing the point. Not only once in fact, I told Him thrice. And you go on teaching 'Trust Allah,' so I trusted. Now don't look at me with anger."

The master said, "Trust in Allah but tether your camel first—because Allah has no other hands than yours."

If He wants to tether the camel He will have to use somebody's hands; He has no other hands. And it is your camel! The best way and the easiest and the shortest way is to use your hands. Trust Allah—don't trust only your hands, otherwise you will become tense. Tether the camel and then trust Allah. You will ask, "Then why trust Allah if you are tethering the camel?"—because a tethered camel can also be stolen. You do whatsoever you can do: that does not make the result certain, there is no guarantee. So you do whatsoever you can, and then whatsoever happens, accept it. This is the meaning of tether the camel: do whatever is possible for you to do, don't shirk your responsibility, and then if nothing happens or something goes wrong, trust Allah. Then He knows best. Then maybe it is right for us to travel without the camel.

It is very easy to trust Allah and be lazy. It is very easy not to trust Allah and be a doer. The third type of man is difficult—to trust Allah and yet remain a doer. But now you are only instrumental; God is the real doer, you are just instruments in His hands.

The Journey

Sorrow and suffering and misery—everything has to be taken non-seriously, because the more seriously you take them, the more difficult it is to get out of them. The more non-serious you are... you can pass through the suffering, through the dark night, singing a song. And if one can pass through the dark night singing a song and dancing, then why unnecessarily torture yourself?

Make this whole journey from here to here just a beautiful laughing matter.

There is a beautiful statement of Mevlana Jalaluddin Rumi, one of the greatest Sufi masters ever. He says:

Come, come, whoever you are;
Wanderer, worshipper, lover of learning...
It does not matter.
Ours is not a caravan of despair.
Come, even if you have broken your vow
A thousand times.
Come, come, yet again come.

The Journey

"Even if you have broken your vow a thousand times..."

Remember this beautiful statement: "Ours is not a caravan of despair." I can also say this. Ours is not a caravan of despair, it is a celebration—it is the celebration of life. People become religious out of misery, and the person who becomes religious out of misery becomes religious for the wrong reasons. And if the very beginning is wrong, the end cannot be right.

Become religious out of joy, out of the experience of beauty that surrounds you, out of the immense gift of life that God has given to you. Become religious out of gratitude, thankfulness. Your temples, your churches, your mosques and *gurudwaras* are full of miserable people. They have turned your temples also into hells. They are there because they are in agony. They don't know God, they have no interest in God; they are not concerned with truth; there is no inquiry. They are just there to be consoled, comforted. Hence they seek anybody who can give them cheap beliefs to patch up their lives, to hide their wounds, to cover up their misery. They are there in search of some false satisfaction.

Ours is not a caravan of despair. It is a temple of joy, of song, of dance, of music, of creativity, of love and life.

It does not matter. You may have broken all the rules—the rules of conduct, the rules of morality. In fact, anybody who has any guts is bound to break those rules.

I agree with Jalaluddin Rumi: he says,

Come, even if you have broken your vow a thousand times.

Intelligent people are bound to break all their vows many times, because life goes on changing, situations go on changing. And the vow is taken under pressure—maybe the fear of hell, the greed for heaven, respectability in society.... It is not coming from your innermost core. When something comes from your own inner being, it is never broken. But then it is never a vow, it is a simple phenomenon like breathing.

Come, come, yet again come!

Everybody is welcome, without any conditions. You do not have to fulfill any requirements.

The time has come when a great rebellion is needed against all established religions. Religiousness is needed in the world but no more religions—no more Hindus, no more Christians, no more Mohammedans—just pure religious people, people who have great respect for themselves.

LAUGHTER

Laughter is eternal, life is eternal, celebration continues. Actors change but the drama continues. Waves change but the ocean continues. You laugh, you change—and somebody else laughs—but laughter continues. You celebrate, somebody else celebrates, but celebration continues. Existence is continuous, it is a continuum. There is not a single moment's gap in it. No death is death, because every death opens a new door—it is a beginning. There is no end to life, there is always a new beginning, a resurrection.

If you change your sadness to celebration, then you will also be capable of changing your death into resurrection. So learn the art while there is still time.

LAUGHTER

THE CHINESE MYSTIC'S LAST SURPRISE

I have heard about three Chinese mystics. Nobody knows their names now, and nobody ever knew their names. They were known only as the "Three Laughing Saints" because they never did anything else; they simply laughed.

These three people were really beautiful - laughing, and their bellies shaking. And then it would become an infection and others would start laughing. The whole marketplace would laugh. When just a few moments before, it was an ugly place where people were thinking only of money, suddenly these three mad people came and changed the quality of the whole marketplace. Now they had forgotten that they had come to purchase and sell. Nobody bothered about greed. For a few seconds a new world opened.

They moved all over China, from place to place, from village to village, just helping people to laugh. Sad people, angry people, greedy people, jealous people—they all started laughing with them. And many felt the key—you can be transformed.

Then, in one village it happened that one of the three died. Village people gathered and they said, "Now there will be trouble. Now we have to see how they laugh. Their friend has died; they must weep." But when they came, the two were dancing, laughing and celebrating the death. The village people said, "Now this is too much. When a man is dead it is profane to laugh and dance." They said, "The whole life we laughed with him. How can we give him the last send-off with anything else?—we have to laugh, we have to enjoy, we have to celebrate. This is the only farewell that is possible for a man who has laughed his whole life. We don't see that he is dead. How can laughter die, how can life die?"

Then the body was to be burned, and the village people said, "We will give him a bath as the ritual prescribes." But those two friends said, "No, our friend has said, 'Don't perform any ritual and don't change my clothes and don't give me a bath. You just put me as I am on the burning pyre.' So we have to follow his instructions."

And then, suddenly, there was a great happening. When the body was put on the fire, that old man had played the last trick. He had hidden many fireworks under his clothes, and suddenly there was a festival! Then the whole village started laughing. These two mad friends were dancing, then the whole village started dancing. It was not a death, it was a new life.

OSHO is a contemporary mystic whose life and teachings have influenced millions of people of all ages, and from all walks of life. He has been described by the *Sunday Times* in London as one of the "1000 Makers of the 20th Century" and by *Sunday Mid-Day* (India) as one of the ten people—along with Gandhi, Nehru and Buddha—who have changed the destiny of India.

About his own work Osho has said that he is helping to create the conditions for the birth of a new kind of human being. He has often characterized this new human being as "Zorba the Buddha"—capable both of enjoying the earthy pleasures of a Zorba the Greek and the silent serenity of a Gautama the Buddha. Running like a thread through all aspects of Osho's work is a vision that encompasses both the timeless wisdom of the East and the highest potential of Western science and technology.

He is also known for his revolutionary contribution to the science of inner transformation, with an approach to meditation that acknowledges the accelerated pace of contemporary life. His unique "Active Meditations" are designed to first release the accumulated stresses of body and mind, so that it is easier to experience the thought-free and relaxed state of meditation.

Osho Commune International, the meditation resort that Osho established in India as an oasis where his teachings can be put into practice, continues to attract some 15,000 visitors per year from more than 100 different countries around the world.

For more information about Osho and his work, including a tour of the meditation resort in Pune, India, visit: **www.osho.com**

The Meditation Resort at Osho Commune International is located about 100 miles southeast of Bombay in Pune, India. Originally developed as a summer retreat for Maharajas and wealthy British colonialists, Pune is now a thriving modern city that is home to a number of universities and high-tech industries.

Osho Commune facilities are spread over 32 acres in a tree-lined suburb known as Koregaon Park. Around 15,000 people from more than 100 different countries visit the resort each year, finding accommodation among a plentiful variety of nearby hotels and private apartments, depending on the length of their stay.

Resort programs are all based in Osho's vision of a qualitatively new kind of human being who is able to participate joyously in everyday life and to relax into silence and meditation. Most programs take place in modern, air-conditioned facilities and include a variety of individual sessions, courses and workshops. Many staff members are world leaders in their respective fields. Program offerings cover everything from creative arts to holistic health treatments, personal growth and therapy, esoteric sciences, the "Zen" approach to sports and recreation, relationship issues and significant life transitions for men and women of all ages. Both individual and group sessions are offered throughout the year, alongside a full daily schedule of Osho's active meditations, and plenty of space for relaxation in the lush tropical gardens, or the pool and court facilities of "Club Meditation."

Outdoor cafes and restaurants within the resort grounds serve both traditional Indian fare and a variety of international dishes made with organically grown vegetables from the commune's own farm. The resort has its own private supply of safe, filtered water.

For information about visiting the resort at Osho Commune International, or to book programs in advance of your visit, call (323) 563-6075 in the USA, or check the **osho.com** website for the "Pune Information Center" nearest you.

Also by Osho

The Book of Secrets
The Osho Zen Tarot
Meditation: The First and Last Freedom
Courage
Creativity
Maturity

Audio

Osho Meditations on Buddhism
Osho Meditations on Sufism
Osho Meditations on Tantra
Osho Meditations on Tao
Osho Meditations on Yoga
Osho Meditations on Zen

For more information:
www.osho.com

A comprehensive web site in different languages, featuring Osho's meditations, books and tapes, an online tour of the meditation resort at Osho Commune International, Osho information centers worldwide, and selections from Osho's talks.

Osho International
New York
Telephone: (1) 212-588-9888
Fax: (1) 212-588-1977
email: osho-int@osho.org